Pierre Joris

Arabia (not so) Deserta

Essays on Maghrebi
&
Mashreqi Writing
&
Culture

SPUYTEN DUYVIL

NEW YORK CITY

© 2019 Pierre Joris
ISBN 978-1-949966-05-3
Cover by Nicole Peyrafitte

Library of Congress Cataloging-in-Publication Data

Names: Joris, Pierre, author.
Title: Arabia (not so) deserta : essays on Maghrebi & Mashreqi writing &
   culture / Pierre Joris.
Description: New York City : Spuyten Duyvil, 2019.
Identifiers: LCCN 2018053144 | ISBN 9781949966053
Subjects: LCSH: Arabic poetry--History and criticism. | Arabic
   poetry--Africa, North--Translations into English. | Arabic
   poetry--Africa--Translations into English. | Arabic poetry--Women
   authors--Translations into English.
Classification: LCC PJ7541 .J525 2019 | DDC 892.7/1009--dc23
LC record available at https://lccn.loc.gov/2018053144

This is a Treasure, a Caravanserai

of a book, erudite, personal, enlightening. Pierre Joris poet, translator, editor, anthologist scholar, flâneur par excellence—is an incomparable and friendly guide to these realms, his lifelong passion and esprit manifest and up for the rigor of this vast deserta. At hand a portable delight and piercing explosion of nomadic poetics with forays into prosody (the riḥlas, and the *Mu'allaqāt*, the hanging poems at the Kaaba (black stone) in Mecca, politics (Arab Spring, see Adonis's comment that Jerusalem is the most "savage city in the world") and culture (a visit to mystic Fez and its living streets), sprinkled with lambent poems of a range of women throughout.

We learn that "troubadour" comes not from "trobare" but from Arabic "tarab" to sing, which suggests a musical poetry that produces an exalted state, and also links to Lorca's "duende" connecting back to Al-Andalus. Anything that gets to the root is good gnosis in these times where, as with all the rest, the intellectual and spiritual battle seems to be with colonial presumption if not genocide. We examine the "melancholic archeology" of many poets including Adonis, Adbellatif Laabi, Mahmoud Darwish, Mohammed Bennis, Habib Tengour. Reference to western authors thickens the mix: Celan, The Beats, Paul Bowles, Charles Olson. If you were someone involved with literary infrastructure, bringing poets and writers of Arabic origin to the US after 9/11 was total anathema. Checkpoints were on "brown alert" and Lynne Cheney had her Campus Watch radar out for subversives here and abroad. This obsessive racism sadly continues under today's US zenophobic policies, only getting worse. Pierre Joris's scintillating Arabia is a salient antidote for our Antithesis Reality.

Anne Waldman

*This one is for Habib Tengour, friend & fellow traveler,
& in memory of Abdelwahab Meddeb.*

Contents

xi   Prologue
Arabic Poetics & the International Literary Scene   1
21   Wallāda bint al-Mustakfi
Homage to Mohammed Khaïr-Eddine   23
29   Ḥafṣa bint al-Hajj Arrakuniyya
For Ghassan Zaqtan   32
35   Fatima Mahmood
Adonis: 1. From Exile to Transgression   38
2. *Extracts from:* Conversations in the Pyrenees   44
50   Fadhila Chabbi
Introduction To *Exile is my Trade: A Habib Tengour Reader*   52
70   Amel Moussa
On Abdelwahab Meddeb   73
78   Mbarka Mint Al-Barra'
Homage to Mohamed Bennis: A Shared Testament.   80
88   Aïcha Mint Chighaly
Prize Fights   91
95   Zahra el Hasnaui Ahmed
On Nabile Farès: 1) Introduction to *A Passenger from the West*   98
2) Breakfast with Nabile Farès   101
104   Mririda N'aït Attik
Abdellatif Laâbi : So many betweens!   107
113   The Song of the Azria
Fez—City through Time & Space   115
125   Chikha Rimitti

On the Nomadic Circulation of Contemporary Poetics		128
	142	Touria Majdouline
Introduction to *Diwan Ifrikiya*		146
	158	Ouidad Benmoussa
On Poetry & Miscegenation: Interview by Orlando Reade		160
	168	Malika el Assimi
Postlude		171
	177	Safaa Fathy
ACKNOWLEDGMENTS		184

Prologue

When I began to gather the materials that would become volume 4 of the *Poems for the Millennium* anthologies, *Diwan Ifrikiya* (renamed by the publisher *The University of California Book of North African Literature*) in the late 80s & 90s, there was a conscious effort to be as inclusive as possible, both in the eras' & areas's various cultural domains, Berber, Arab & beyond, as well as in matters of gender. Trying to bring to the fore the work of women poets was not an easy task, as in a culture where oral poetry had always been & was still very present & alive, the gender of the "author" of an orally transmitted poem, song or narrative is often not easily ascertained. Simultaneously, work published in print under a woman's signature was sparse, be it for the older periods the book covered or even for the modern era. Happily, in exactly the two decades spanning our gathering activity this began to change & many more women writers saw their work become publicly available. And yet, despite our care, the result is still not reassuring: 27 women as against 180 men.

In order to leaven the all-too male focus of the essays gathered here, I am framing them with a range of Maghrebi women's voices taken from *Diwan Ifrikiya*, in an attempt both to give these still not visible & audible enough poets more exposure while deterritorializing my own gaze via multiple lines of flight pointing to the future. These poets will be presented with one or several shorter poems (or extracts from a larger work) & the accompanying commentary, thus in the same format in which they appeared in *Diwan Ifrikiya*. Their reach in time is from 11C Al-Andalus to 20C Morocco. I selected all of them from among the Arabic-language practitioners whose work, for reasons of translation, is as yet less available on this side of the Atlantic than that of their francophone sisters.

Arabic Poetics
& the International Literary Scene

[Note: this lecture took place September 19, 2001, thus a week after September 11, 2001 at Naropa University, Boulder, CO]

It is good to be here. I was pleased when the skies opened wider & New York State receded... when I saw the wide open spaces of this part of America, it felt as if a load started to lift off my shoulders for the first time since September 11—nine days that feel like a year. Obviously I have not sat down in these nine days to write out a lecture, so this is what the French would call a talk *à batons rompus*—an expression coming either from a way of hitting a drum alternately in a sort of broken rhythm that is not a roll, or from a tapestry design of stick-like lines around a central motif. A talk, then, about a range of matters but a tapestry through which the New York City events will doubtlessly wind their way.

First of all, I am pleased to be here because in my thinking through the events of the past week there are two people I tried to think with & through: they are Allen Ginsberg & William Burroughs. It was Allen who years ago taught me about the need to think or write at times through somebody else's mind. I think there was an occasion for this this past week, thinking through Allen's mind in terms of compassion, in terms of trying to see what one can do without anger, while trying to keep a compassionate mind. And of course Burroughs is extremely useful to think through exactly such catastrophic events; for me he has the most penetrating political mind of any writer of the second part of the 20th century.

I was going to speak on the nomadic aspects of what I think of as the most adventurous poetry worldwide; but I am going to restrict myself, for obvious reasons, to an area & culture much in the news, much reviled while little known—but that should, exactly now, be studied deeply: Arab poetry & Arab culture. Maybe this brief talk can help in some small measure to widen our knowledge & appreciation of this culture allowing us a wider & deeper, & thus more sympathetic, view, so that we do not fall into the kind of stupid "Bushisms" we have been assaulted by of late.

Last week at the State University where I work, SUNY Albany, we held teach-ins because most of my students are from New York City or Long Island, & the events of September 11 were very rough on them. Most of these undergraduates don't have much knowledge of history—& thus also lack any way to think through & place such a catastrophic event. With this in mind William Kennedy, the novelist & founder of the New York State Writers' Institute at SUNY Albany, & I did a reading of sorts. Kennedy read from a historical book citing Truman's diaries of the moments before the atom bomb was dropped followed by witness accounts from Hiroshima & Nagasaki. I read a text by the Palestinian poet Mahmoud Darwish, from a book called *Memory for Forgetfulness*, which is the memoir he kept during 1982 in Beirut, when Beirut was being shelled daily by Israel. This is from the opening pages of that book:

> *"Out of one dream another dream is born...*
> *—Are you well? I mean are you alive?*
> *—How did you know I was just this moment laying my head on your knee to sleep?*
> *—Because you woke me up when you stirred in my belly. I knew then I was your coffin. Are you alive? Can you hear me?*
> *—Does it happen much, that you are awakened from one dream by another, itself the interpretation of the dream?*
> *—Here it is, happening to you and to me. Are you alive?*
> *—Almost.*

—And have the devils cast their spell on you?
—I don't know, but in time there's room for death.
—Don't die completely.
—I'll try not to.
—Don't die at all.
—I'll try not to.
—Tell me, when did it happen? I mean, when did we meet? When did we part?
—Thirteen years ago.
—Did we meet often?
—Twice: once in the rain, and again in the rain. The third time, we didn't meet at all. I went away and forgot you. A while ago I remembered. I remembered I'd forgotten you. I was dreaming.
—That also happens to me. I too was dreaming. I had your phone number from a Swedish friend who'd met you in Beirut. I wish you good night! Don't forget not to die. I still want you. And when you come back to life, I want you to call me. How the time flies! Thirteen years! No. It all happened last night. Good night!

* * *

Three o'clock. Daybreak riding on fire. A nightmare coming from the sea. Roosters made of metal. Smoke. Metal preparing a feast for metal the master, & a dawn that flare sup in all the senses before it breaks. A roaring that chases me out of bed & throws me into this narrow hallway. I want nothing, & I hope for nothing. I can't direct my limbs in this pandemonium. No time for caution, & no time for time. If I only knew—if I knew how to organize the crush of this death that keeps pouring forth. If only I knew how to liberate the screams held back in a body that no longer feels like mine from the sheer effort spent to save itself in this uninterrupted chaos of shells. "Enough!"

"Enough!" I whisper to find out if I can still do anything that will guide me to myself & point to the abyss opening in six directions. I can't surrender to this fate, & I can't resist it. Steel that howls, only to have other steel bark back. The fever of metal is the song of this dawn. (...)

Memory for Forgetfulness (published by the University of California Press) is a tremendous memoir by one of the great contemporary writers, Mahmoud Darwish. Some of his poetry has been translated[1]. If the early work is more profoundly & maybe essentially political in terms of creating a Palestinian identity in midst of the disaster that befell his people, his later work expands to encompass wider cultural concerns, as he tries to write of & through the culture of the Mediterranean, & specifically its Arab contribution via the cultures of al-Andalus. This is something we in the West know very little about, & that is definitely a major lack—& a shame.

A strong tradition of poetry is not only core to Arab culture (until the 20th century it is the essential genre of literature) but tremendous in its achievements. On the plane over when I had a quiet moment (I was looking around to make sure nobody was seeing it, I was afraid someone might call the marshal) I was reading a book that came in the mail a couple weeks ago called *Peaks of Yemen I Summon* by the anthropologist Steven Caton. It is an ethnopoetics study of Yemeni tribal poetry, clearly demonstrating—as do a number of other books I have read on this matter—that the role of poetry in tribal Yemeni society is still core to the society's socio-political dynamic. That is, all events that make up the weave of the social life, get vocalized & often realized through poems—be these marriages or wars. War, for instance, can get

---

[1] By now (2019) there are many of Darwish's books of poetry available in English. Check out *A River Dies of Thirst, In the Presence of Absence, Journal of an Ordinary Grief, Why did you Leave this Horse Alone?*, all published by Archipelago books. Darwish died in 2008.

calmed down. War in such a tribal setting can often be faked, i.e. performed symbolically by verbal & /or gestural jousts, to some extent: this is not how we Westerners, weaned on the Lawrence of Arabia fiction, imagine things to be. Caton describes a tribal war situation where there was shooting indeed, & then people were asking him to bring them something. When he said, how can I, they answered, look, those shots missed by three feet, this is only a show, for honor—in half an hour we are going to talk. And they did so, through poems—improvised yet very formal poems. Nearly everything can be put into a poem, making poems still a major form of political & social discourse.

This has been going on for a couple millennia. We have very famous poems from pre-Islamic times, the seven odes known as the *Mu'allaqāt*, i.e. the "hanging ones" because they were supposedly stitched on cloth that was hung from the *Ka'ba*, the big black stone in Mecca. Later on, with the arrival of the third monotheism, Islam, when the more purely religious elements took over they replaced these hangings with verses from the *Quran*. Those seven odes are extremely complex poems—& I would have loved to see someone like Louis Zukofsky, maybe our greatest formal genius, do an extra section of *A* that would have brought something of this great work over into English via adaptation/translation into complex European forms. The *Mu'allaqāt* are nearly untranslatable for us, because American poetry in this century, from Pound on, has worked at cutting away rhetorical blubber, something that was necessary to get us out of late 19th century Victorian verse & find a language that was usable in & accurate for our modern industrial & now post-industrial condition.

For centuries, classical Arab poetry worked on a very rich rhetorical level while at the same time being extremely formal. You have totally determined stress patterns, you have inimitable mono-rhyme structures that could stretch over 100 lines & /or a whole ode, something we obviously cannot do in English. The translations that we have are mainly 19th century British, i.e. colonial translations, & they are awful to our ears because they sound exactly like bad late Victorian or Tennysonian orientalism. There is a huge job to be done in this field—to bring all of those major poems back into our present. Basil Bunting did some excellent work in this direction, with his translation/adaptations of poems by Firdausi & Rudaki in what he called his "Overdrafts"—though those are Persian poets. But most translations of this kind of work have been limp-languaged, fake mystical things—vide the various versions of Rumi we are stuck with. In French, on the other hand, it has recently been shown that such rhetoric based translations can still be viable: a profoundly worked, complexly syntaxed, rhetorically-mimetic translation of the *Mu'allaqāt* was proposed by Jacques Berque, one of the greatest Maghrebi scholars of the 20th century—born of French parents in North Africa, & who passed just recently in France. He was able to reproduce this classical Arabic rhetoric in a very complex but gorgeously written French by transforming it into a, how to say, post-Mallarmean may be the best word, syntactical structure so complex that it never falls into easy Hugolian alexandrines.

A number of years ago—in 78 or 79—I tried to translate one of the odes with the help of an Iraqi poet friend exiled to Algeria (where I was living & teaching at the time) because the Iraqi government wanted to hang him for being a member of the Communist party. When I began asking him about the *Mu'allaqāt* & the pre-islamic tradition of poetry, he said "oh, my father had a second-hand book shop in Bagdad, filled with old scrolls & manuscripts. I know these poems—we all know them—by heart, the seven odes, & we love to recite them, as that is the way they live again, they were oral poems made to be spoken or sung." I told Mohammed that I was really interested in Ibn Tarafa's Ode, because Tarafa was, from what I had been able to glean, the wildest of those seven poets, & to me very Rimbaud-like—always walking on "the wild side," he was independent & a rebel against the state, & eventually arrested for insulting a king who sent him on a treacherous mission where, caught, he was given the choice of how to die. He said, fill me with wine, then leave me in the sand, bleeding out through the holes you'll make in me like a goat-skin water bag—& that's how he went, very young, in his twenties. His ode is gorgeous. With Mohammed's help we created an interlinear literal version which I then needed to fashion into a readable contemporary poem in English. When I tried to work this out, the need to cut out the rhetoric made me try to pass the text through a Japanese mode, the haiku, or rather the renga, though one with a William Carlos Williams twist, namely his three-step lines, which indeed allowed me to cut away the rhetorical language-husks, leaving just image kernels. In a way it is a totally unfaithful translation but it was truly the only way that I could think of doing it & coming out with a viable poem.

Let me read you from this ode:

Khawla's abandoned camp site :
    an old tattoo's fading glow
        on the schist slopes of Thamad mountain

        Between brown lips her smile
      mirrors marigolds unfolding in white sand
          on a dew-wet dune

the sun lent it its rays—black antinomy
    darkened her gums
  never touched a tooth

If you look for me among the assembled sages
    you'll find me — you'll find me too
in the taverns where they sell wine

When late at night she sings for us
my illustrious companions's faces
light up like novas

Come off it! you who tell me
not to fight & not to fuck,
if

ever I did quit,
could you offer me
immortality?

As you cannot save me from death
let me offer death, right now, all
this hand can hold.

I wouldn't give a damn
to know the hour of my death
if it weren't for these three:

first — & quit bugging me about it —
the pleasure of an old wine that
foams as soon as you add water

then there is the call from someone in need:
I come running, hunched over, a
tamarisk wolf sensing water

& last but not least the joy in shortening a cloudy day
laying a well-fleshed lady
under a firmly pitched tent.

> *I have spent my life generously drinking*
>   *at its source . if death should come tomorrow*
>   *whose throat would be parched?*
>
> *No matter how fast a man runs*
>   *death is a long leash*
>   *its other end firmly grasped*
>
> *& the days will lay bare what you don't yet know*
>   *& someone will refuse you bread*
>   *someone will come*
>
>   *bringing news:*
>   *a traveller with no luggage*
>   *& no invitation.*

Now this tradition of the ode, the qacida, as it is called in Arabic, is still alive today—is still seen as the foremost model of Arabic poetry, from or against which you have to write, even all the way through the 20th century. You'll see it resurface in the last poem I'll read by one of the great contemporary Algerian avant-gardista poets. Now, the critical-scholarly tradition, for good & bad, has also survived through the ages. In the 8th, 9th, & 10th centuries—the early centuries of Islamic culture—there were incredibly intelligent & fastidious scholars who wrote great treatises on poetics, often Aristotelian in inspiration, but often also improvements on Aristotle, with an interesting feel of modernity, in fact, in terms of elegance of classification & formalization. Those books have held sway over the centuries, & like Aristotle & Horace, are still read & studied today. In a way it was very difficult to break out of that mode—just as in the West until very recently, the core literary values were based on Aristotle, Horace

& Longinus.[2]

Unhappily the West has been very negative about the Arab poetic traditions, either ignoring it totally or touting its supposed backwardness (even when glorifying, à la Lawrence—of Arabia, not D.H.—its antique achievements). An interesting story showing how far such denials & misconstructions can go, has to do with the European lyric tradition, which, as we have all learned from Pound & others, goes right back to the *troubadours*, in Provence, where the first lyric poems were composed. After a hundred years it disappeared, but before that Europeans had some epic writings, such as the Occitan *Cançon d'Antioquia* or the Old French *Chanson de Roland*, basically old tribal epic, i.e. a nasty or glorious world seen by males: I, boy, beat up on you, boy. But the lyric, the love song, comes from the *troubadours*. Since the Middle Ages, the root of the very word *troubadours*, our philologists have told us, comes from *trobar* which means, they say, "to find" in Latin. Now if you look *trobar* up in the etymological dictionary, it has a little star on it that means this is a suggested root, this is not a documented root of this word. If you ask any specialist in Arabic poetry, specifically in Arabic Spain, the Moorish kingdom, that root is in fact "tarab," the Arabic word for "song." There is no question that that is where it came from. But even now, in 2001, philological discussions of this matter keep going on, with the best European—German & French & Spanish & English philologists—unable to tear themselves loose from what at base is cultural imperialism, namely their belief that there has to be European roots, an autochthonous European origin to lyric poetry & that it may—must—not come via Arabic song & poetry. But that is indeed where this lyrical tradition that will also give us Dante & beyond, comes from.

---

2 Some of this early Arabic—at least the Maghrebian material—has been reproduced in the "Invention of prose" section of my (& Habib Tengour's) recent anthology *The University of California Book of North African Literature* (volume 4 in the Poems for the Millennium series).

If we now have a look at what is happening with Arabic poetry, a quick overview would suggest there was, belatedly, i.e. well after European modernism, the beginning of an Arab modernism. This can be linked to a specific group of poets in Beirut around the magazine *Shi'r*—which means poetry—namely, Yusuf al-Khal, Unsi el Hage, Adonis, & a few more, who, indeed, read Eliot & a range of twentieth-century French poetry in the early 1950s. *The Wasteland*'s mythopoeic materials sent some of these poets back to their own mythopoeic past to look for inspiration & matters of spiritual rebirth, & also, via French modernism, forward to free verse experiments. Adonis, for example, originally Ali Ahman Said, took his name from the ancient fertility god. These poets began breaking down the classical norms of Arabic poetry, as represented by the highly formal *Qacida* structure. These experiments would eventually spread to other countries of the Mashreq.

But one more word on the idea of "belated:" If you ask Adonis, it is the European modernism of the late 19C (Baudelaire, urban poetry, Whitman, formal innovation, etc.) that is belated—from a wider, non-Eurocentric, view of things. He points to the great Baghdadi poets & thinkers of the 10-11C, such as Abu Nuwas & Abu Tammam, or Omar Khayyam, & al-Rawandi & al-Razi as thinkers & theoreticians, & to the nature of visionary experience by the Sufi mystics, to locate a modernist, i.e. urban, experimental in both form & content, anti-traditional, sexually adventurous, stance leading to "the emergence of new truths about man & the world—[which] is not only a criticism of the ancient but also a refutation of it."[3] It is still difficult for us to see this, or realize it, because again, somebody like Omar Khayyam has been killed over & over again by bad translation, giving us a kind of easy, new age-y Orientalist pap; on top of this we don't have the cultural context available, i.e. we lack the necessary information to be able to see the ways in which he & these other poets & thinkers were revolutionary.

---

3 Adonis, *An Introduction to Arab Poetics*, Saqi Books, London, 1990, p. 78.

Simultaneously, throughout the Arab world, you also had & still have an ongoing, lively tradition of oral, demotic poetry of songs & proverbs & tales, even epics, relatively formalized, as such literatures usually are. This, by the way, is one of the features of Arabic culture that fascinates me deeply: while in Europe, after Gutenberg, the oral tradition rather quickly died out, in the Arab world, both written & oral traditions have maintained themselves for 2000 years, enriching the one the other in the process. So, even if the written tradition, after the Baghdadi modernism, suffered a setback in that the conservatives & reactionaries took over, & much of the production grew, if not stale, then repetitive, poetry stayed alive as the major form language arts took in the Arab world. As already mentioned, it is the *Shi'r* poets who broke the heave, to quote Pound. They began writing—and here is something, when you read them, something to watch out for, the term, they call them prose poems, but it is not the Baudelairian & 20C Euro-american prose poem set as a block of justified prose. The Arab prose poem can be freely all over the page with various line breaks; what makes it "prose" in the sense of an Arabic poetics is that it simply does not follow the old forms, eschewing the classical tight & formal metrics (though it may even still rhyme at times). It is really what we would call free verse.

So indeed there is a very strong modernist movement that emerges in the 1950s from Beirut, as a center, but also from the wider Middle East. And this is very interesting to think about even now, when we are getting saturated by our media with these images of a medieval-looking world, where nothing is modern, we are shown these rural backwards Arabs & told that in Afghanistan & elsewhere, all that they, these people want is America, everybody wants America & its gadgets. Unhappily the disinformation about those parts of the world is rampant, & will only be made worse by the events in New York.

So there is a pitch here also for people who are here today—you're still young & have the ability to learn a language like Arabic. There is a huge amount of work to be done in terms of what needs to be brought into our language [English] from that language, or that needs to be done anew. Translation always needs to be done anew. In a way every generation has to translate the major texts again for itself. When you have a situation like the one in relation to Arabic poetry where you have two hundred years of bad translation (there are of course major exceptions to this), the job is even more urgent. Bad translation can kill a poet for a whole generation in a country or for a culture. Take a poet from any language you are not familiar with & read him or her in what a knowledgeable person could tell you is a bad translation. For example, I recently came across someone advertised as a major Czech poet, so I got the one translated book available & the work in English sounded like bad Robert Pinksy so I just couldn't go on & put the book down—that poet's work may never again be visible for me. So as a translator there is a responsibility you have & should be aware of.

My own work in this area—except for Tarafa & some other work I have translated in collaboration with a native speaker, not my favorite method of translation,—has been poetry from another center of Arabo-Berber culture namely from the Maghreb, that is, Tunisia, Algeria, & Morocco. These countries gained independence in the early 1960s, & given the strictures of French Colonialism it was forbidden to speak Arabic in whatever schools there were for the quote natives unquote. I remember people telling me how as kids in grade school in Algeria in the 1950s they would be fined the equivalent of a dime if, during a break, they were caught speaking Arabic, even among themselves. So you have several generations of poets for whom French was the available cultural language, who had to write in French, & who are writing brilliantly in French. There are a several beautiful texts in English by a Moroccan, Abdelkebir Khatibi. One of these, titled "Love in Two Languages," came out in the mid 1990s. Khatibi has this ideal vision that every poem should be written in two languages, at least, which of course speaks to me as a poet very much. Every poem should be written in all languages simultaneously. Here's how he puts this:

> Yes, I spoke, I grew up around the Only One & the Name, & the Book of my invisible god should have ended within me. Extravagant second thought that stays with me always. The idea imposes itself as I write it: every language should be bi-lingual! The asymmetry of body & language, of speech & writing—at the threshold of the untranslatable.

In Maghrebi literature we have a vast amount of first rate work. I could read for the next three hours... By the way, a magazine people should look at is called *Banipal*, an amazingly rich magazine of Arab literature that comes out of London. Its drawback—it translates poems both from Arabic & from French, so from Maghrebian & Mashreqian literatures—some of its translators come from a rather more middle of the road American or English tradition so the poems wind up being closer to what we usually call confessional poetry, what we might call the Iowa tradition. So there are some translation problems to be kept in mind. But it is a very useful magazine if you want to find out what is being written now in a range of Arab countries.

I'm going to read a few extracts. Ounsi el Hage is one of the great 1950s poets, born in Lebanon in 1937, both poet & journalist. There is in fact a great tradition among Arab poets to be journalists & writers at the same time, & there is a great tradition of Arabic newspapers publishing poems. My first poems translated into Arabic appeared in *Al Quds* which is the Arabic daily published in London that goes into those Arabic countries that will let it in on a given day, because it is politically independent. The cultural editor is a Jordanian Bedouin poet, Amjad Nasser.

It's wonderful to get the morning paper, & with it, as you unfold it, a whole page of poems. Again, this goes back to what I said earlier as to how poetry still is of core importance in this culture. Here is a poem by Ounsi el Hage, written in the 1960s. I'll read an extract, translated by Brandel France, from the long poem, "The Messenger With Her Hair Long to the Springs," a kind of reworking of the genesis story:

This is the story of the other side of creation
I discovered it, my eyes obscured
The path, my beloved,
Leads from her awaiting me
Leads from my return to her
This is the story of the other side of creation
Listen
Do not shoot the doors
The breakers bear the message to the wind
The wind to the trees
The trees to notebooks.
You, old men with homes, & you, young boys of the streets
Sit this very night in the presence of the lover.
You, who hurry about, did you really leave only to return?
Shatter the night for an instant
Come, gather round the one to testify.
Pray, my love, that I spread a feast, befitting their appetite.
Birds of the harvest season soar past
But your light does not recede, its hand before me still.
I am the collector of your echo's traces
Read me before they know me, then I will arrive early at the heart
This, in my twisted language, in your vision
This, in my thieving hands, is your treasure
This, from my row boat, is your sea, so watch over your sea from my boat, your eyes the sails that protect me

You, who change life with crushing ignorance
You are the dependable one
You change life, effortless
With the nakedness of purity, to its passion alone do secrets yield
This is your story
The story of the other side of creation

Thinking of the old myths & stories I wanted to read one, maybe two texts. A good friend puts out a magazine in Paris called *Arapoetica*. He is an Iraqi in exile for thirty years, the last of the great surrealists, a total wild man of poetry, called Abdel Kader El Janabi. Here is the first text, translated by me, called "Against Ibn Arabi:"

> Here I am all alone, quarreling with the age, both feet kicking the jugs of Being. Night vibrates with a litany of shadowless reflections. From its window the Absolute in profile contemplates its confines: the celestial sounds propagate through the old pond where metal & loam, past & ends, bone & vocable come to slake their thirst. Mud explodes & consciousness sails against the current. In this immense opacity of contemplation where air is the anticipation of darkness, I see the singular rise in multiples from the bottom of the amphora & wait in the cold of the real to be smashed.
>
> No need to step into a sea at the edge of which the prophets came to a halt, or crack open the world's safe, for man to be the knot of creation & keep in his hands the Seal of future treasures. Creative in each one of us, the spark, no longer hoping to unite with the fires of heaven, becomes flame, spark of itself, mother of all ignitions, new lands. A drop flees the ocean, becomes ocean. The universe holds out a hand to the ephemeral.

One of the great Moroccan poets with a recently published book in English translation is Abdellatif Laâbi.[4] He published one of the great avant-garde magazines, *Souffles*, from 1966 until 1972, which is on the web[5] now, for which he was arrested & jailed; he spent six years in prison under the regime of king Hassan II for being a revolutionary threat. He has been in Paris since his release. I used one of his poems as an epigraph to one of my books. This poem goes:

> I'm not the nomad
> searches for the well
> the sedentary has dug,
> I drink little water
> and walk
> apart from the caravan.

I want to close by reading a poem—or an extract at least—by Habib Tengour, the Algerian poet, from one of his great works, which I published in translation as a chap book called *Empedokles's Sandal*.[6] It presents itself *ab initio* in an astoundingly wide nomadicity: the author's name clearly locates him as an Arab, the title refers to a Greek philosopher situated in Italy & the epigraph cites a nineteenth century German poet, Friedrich Hölderlin. There is Poundian or post-Poundian modernity visibly at work here, confirmed by the poem itself, which reads as a modernist textual montage / collage of a wide-ranging array mixing the personal & the historical. The opening lines set the tone of contem-

---

[4] Since 2001, there have been a number of books by Abdellatif Laâbi published in English translation; see also pp. 25-26, 106-109, 122, 158, 168-170

[5] http://clicnet.swarthmore.edu/souffles/sommaire.html

[6] A full volume of Tengour's work came out in 2012: *Exile is My Trade: A Habib Tengour Reader* edited, introduced & translated by Pierre Joris (Black Widow Press).

poraneity, down to the slashes used to separate the word-shards. Then, paradoxically, the poem starts with the word "stop." It took me awhile to realize that this is a reference to the classical ode motif of the atlal, the first stanza of the poem in which the poet stops his mount at the site of last year's campfire—& then realized that the whole of the very post-modern poem is ghosted by the structure of the most classical of Arab poems, the ghazal, or ode. Here it is:

Traces/ Renown/ Shades/ Urns/ Life(s)/ Epoch/ Zenith
Lucid/ Strangely/ Suspended

Stop
a pause of short duration   the closed
space   compelled remembrances tears
they are not necessary
the dictionary tempers the banality of the stereotype
a nostalgia emerges in the description of the place

like a circumscribed exile
like the eye dimming after the junction

handicap of the code
unusual names at night fall
despite the invocation's depth
the usages intermingle on the asphalt
the trace vainly sought   there   effaced
it is visible
             o heart you weaver
the times don't change that fast their duration
nor the embrace that follows where a soul decyphers itself
a proliferation of signs but

                    the loud voice the one
that unties the tongues & curbs the discourse
alas
        so many lethal traps on the way
the angels refuse to accompany us
the lights blink ostentatiously
the harangues lead us far from the encampment

This is the moment

to enter subreptitously I go in
my purpose my utterance to open the door
to sayunder the dictation of a continuous effusion
to align a text without history
for a moment to enjoy the stopping
to reveal the splendor & brilliance of the vestiges
without giving in to the letter's subterfuges

Paris november rue Saint-Antoine Constantine
cité du 20 août Paris again
examine each of these addresses
a small light rift whips the clouds

Itinerary
of precise annotations the return therein
envisaged I know
the tracings the dwellings & the hunger
the hesitation to take to the road is real

renown by auction
victims interrogate who kills & reason

pomp makes sense only if sustained
a hollow word illusions
charisma is not a copyright trademark
danger metamorphoses the limbs
there is nothing to brag about today

(...)

Shukran. Thank you.

WALLĀDA BINT AL-MUSTAKFI (CORDOBA 994-1091):
Four Poems

By Allah, I'm made for higher goals & I walk with grace & style.
I blow kisses to anyone but reserve my cheeks for my man.

***

If you were faithful to our love you wouldn't have lost your head over my maid.
You dropped a branch in full bloom for a lifeless twig.
You know I am the moon yet you fell for a tiddly star.

***

Ibn Zaidūn, in spite of his qualities, is unkind to me for no reason.
He looks at me menacingly as if I'd come to unman his boyfriend Ali.

***

Ibn Zaidūn, though a man of quality, loves the unbent rods in men's trousers.
If he saw a joystick dangling from a palm tree he'd fly after it like a craving bird.

translated by Abdullah al-Udhari

COMMENTARY

Wallada bint al-Mustakfi was the daughter of Muhammad III of Cordoba, one of the last Umayyad Cordoban caliphs, who came to power in 1024 after assassinating the previous caliph & who was assassinated himself two years later. Her early childhood passed during the high period of the Cordoban Caliphate while her adolescence came during the tumultuous period following the eventual succession of Sanchuelo, who in his attempts to seize power from Hisham II plunged the caliphate into civil war. As Muhammad III had no male heir, Wallada inherited his properties, & used them to open a palace & literary hall in Córdoba. She was an ideal beauty of the time: blonde, fair-skinned & blue-eyed, in addition to being intelligent, cultured & proud. She also was somewhat controversial, walking out in public without a hijab. The first verse of the first poem above was written on the righthand side of the front of her robe, & the second verse on the lefthand side. The love of her life was the poet Ibn Zaydun.

Homage to Mohammed Khaïr-Eddine

Tous ceux d'ici qui se réclament de l'avant-garde se leurrent. L'avant-garde c'est tout ce qui se fait en Afrique.
—Mohammed Khair-Eddine

For a long time the only West I knew was the Wild West. Raised in a small country between France & Belgium & Germany, in that post-World War II era one could accurately describe as an American cultural quasi-protectorate, Indians & cowboys was my West. What I later learned to call the Maghreb was East or South. And yet there were intimations. One of my earliest haptic memories is a word, a name, I heard on the news my father was listening to on the mahagony Nordmende radio set with the large green eye. It was the name: Krim Bel Kacem. I can still hear it in the singing French inflections of the news announcer—coming back over & over: Krim Bel Kacem, Krim Bel Kacem. A few years later I found out the connection between the name & a historical reality: visiting Paris with my father, staying at the Hotel du Brésil near the Luxembourg gardens, I was woken in the middle of the night by several loud explosions & the rattatatat of machine gun fire. The next day I learned that this was an OAS *plastiquage* & the ensuing getaway. Through the sounds of the last reactionary spasms of the Algerian war of independence, the history of the Maghreb had entered my life.

By 1965 I was living in Paris, studying medicine in the rue des Saints Pères during the day & hanging out in St. Michel, the new hip quarter, at night, reading voraciously in Shakespeare & Co., the English language bookshop on rue de la Bûcherie, & beginning to write. That year I dropped out of medical school, having decided to devote myself completely to poetry. Cut off financially by my parents, I needed a place to live & asked George Whitman if I could stay in one of the upstairs rooms of the bookshop. No problem, George said, & that afternoon I moved my suitcase into the small upstairs room with the two mattresses. Evenings I worked selling the New York Times in Montparnasse, & when I came back late that night, I slipped into the room & onto my cot as silently as possible so as not to wake up the roommate who was already sleeping on the other mattress. I woke when my companion started moving about the room, swung my legs sideways, sat on the cot & greeted him, introducing myself. He looked up briefly from the book he had started to read, returned the greeting & introduced himself: Mohammed Khaïr-Eddine.

What has remained with me from that moment on through all subsequent meetings with Mohammed Khaïr-Eddine can be summed up in one word: intensity. A fierce intensity or an intense fierceness—it was often impossible to decide which it was. Here was someone totally gathered around, or rather, *in* a single point of focus, from inside out: a solar intensity radiating from somewhere deep inside, or better, gathering from *everywhere* inside (soul & skin, organs & bones, mind & blood) to radiate out through a gaze that concentrated the black sun of the interior, twin to the desert sun of his birth place. Black suns, may be more accurate, or as he put it in an early poem: "My black blood contains a thousand suns."

I was in awe of him, who was five years older & had already published one small pamphlet, *Nausée Noire*, which had come out in 1964 as a special edition of the magazine *siècle à mains* in London. I treasure my copy of it, especially the stark black cover on which a little white lets through the title & the author's name, & the small typewriter font that demands a near painful concentration of the reader's gaze. (I have to add that years later the poet Claude Royet-Journoud, who had published the pamphlet, complained to me that M K-E had not given *siècle à mains* credit when the poem was reprinted in the volume *Soleil Arachnide*. My guess is that Mohammed had no time for such niceties in his frenzied rush ahead.)

I saw him off & on during the next six months, sometimes at our home *cum* library, sometimes in local bars around St Michel. He was broke most of the time, despite the fact that, as I learned later, George Whitman would help him out financially on occasion while Jean-Paul Sartre gave him a small monthly allowance—that never lasted more than a week or two. I was making a little money selling the *Times,* most of which went into bottles of cheap red wine, often shared with Mohammed. It was on those occasions that I first learned about Maghrebian literature, that the names of Kateb Yacine & Nedjma, of Abdellatif Laâbi & the magazine *Souffles,* & many others first came to my attention. A world I did not know of had begun to open up then & is still doing so, today.

Khaïr-Eddine was not talkative, though wine would loosen him up for awhile & he could become expansive, only to just as quickly withdraw again, or, at times, turn querulous—he didn't suffer fools gladly, & my ignorance must have made me look the fool all too often in those days. But what has remained core for me, more so than the literary & political information gathered from him, was the example his intensity set: he was the poet incarnate, a truly rimbaldian figure whose total dedication to his art awed me no end. I was still searching, unsure of myself, unsure that it was even possible for someone to become a poet in a language that was not the mother-tongue, unsure if I could bear the absolute exile such a decision implied. Khaïr-Eddine was living proof that it was possible & that total dedication to the chosen path was the only way to achieve this aim. Years later Allen Ginsberg mentioned in conversation that he often tried to think "through" others, through their minds (he mentioned Kerouac of course, but also Robert Creeley & Robert Kelly, as well as others that don't come to mind right now). I immediately thought how often I had tried in those early years to think "through" Mohammed Khaïr-Eddine's mind—both in order to try & understand it

& its path through poetry, & in order to gather from it the courage to continue the trek.

And the trek did continue: in 1967 I left Paris for New York & didn't return for a longer stay for many years, except for quick 1 or 2 day forays on which I didn't see Khaïr-Eddine, though I would get news from him via his books which I would buy on those visits. By the late seventies I was living in Algeria & one spring day, I believe it was in '79, waking up in a hotel in Tizi-Ouzou I went down for breakfast & over coffee flicking lackadaisically through the pages of *El Moujahid* I was startled to come across an article relating Khaïr-Eddine's arrest in Morocco. He hadn't been able to bear his exile any longer & had tried to go home, rejoin his beloved "Suddique" though knowing full well that his 15 year long public rant against the king & the Moroccan government would get him into trouble. I truly feared for his life then, knowing the hardships Laâbi & many others had undergone during their years in jail. There was not much I could do, except write letters to the editor & sign petitions demanding his immediate release. Many of us did so, & there was enough pressure generated to set him free.

Some time later I was coming through Paris to do a reading with a number of American poets at the Centre Américain on the Boulevard Raspail. After the readings we all went for dinner to the Coupole on the Boulevard Montparnasse. It was a grand & festive poets' table, including Allen Ginsberg, William Burroughs, Kathy Acker, Gregory Corso as well as a number of French poets. We were in the middle of our repast when I looked up & saw someone come through the door. I immediately recognized Mohammed Khaïr-Eddine, & was about to get up & go over & embrace him, but something held me back. He had changed since I last saw him, nearly fifteen years before: aged, of course, as we all had, but he looked haggard, haunted. What had not changed was the intensity, the fierceness. He walked in & made his way between the tables, clearly looking for someone but unable to find that person. When he came close to our table, his gaze finally locked with mine. I raised my arms & yelled over the din: "Mohammed, it's me, Pierre! How are you?" He acknowledged the greeting with a quick nod of the head, came closer & said fiercely: "Give me a hundred francs!"

I noticed then that several waiters & a maître-d'hôtel were closing in, had in fact kept a close watch on Mohammed's progress through the restaurant—they obviously knew him & had their orders. Mohammed ignored them with total disdain & repeated his demand. "Sure, but why don't you sit down & have a drink with us," I said, motioning to a waiter to pull up a chair "pour mon ami." The waiter glanced at the maître d'h, who glanced at our motley table, shrugged his shoulders & nodded an okay to the waiter, who took a chair from an near-by empty table & started to bring it over. Mohammed turned & waved him away: "Non." Then he turned back to me, reiterating his demand. I tried once more: "Mohammed, look, sit down, drink & have dinner with us—I would like you to meet Allen Ginsberg & William Burroughs and..." He interrupted me: "Non, I have things to do. *Donne-moi cent francs!*" I realized that he was locked into something only he knew about, & that I would not be able to make him budge. I gave him the money, he nodded a thank you, we shook hands, he turned heel & disappeared into the night outside. I had an urge to get up & run after him, but didn't, realizing that I could not join him where he was going. So I turned to my neighbor, Kathy Acker, & started to tell her everything I knew about Mohammed Khaïr-Eddine, what an absolutely superb poet he was, the greatest of his generation in Morocco, how powerful his prose was, how violently he had disemboweled the colonizer's language in order to be able to put it to accurate new uses, how he had turned it into a truly alive counter-language & how especially in *Moi, l'Aigre* he had done that with a brilliance that bordered on genius. I sang Mohammed's praises for as long as she & anyone else at the table would listen—I wanted them to know, but, maybe before all, I wanted to reassure myself, as I knew without knowing it, that this was the last time I would see him. And it was. Except that from time to time when I sit down to write a poem I try to think through him, Mohammed Khaïr-Eddine, & try to gather that way some of the absolute intensity & fearlessness necessary for a true *guérilla poétique*.

When I heard of his death, the line of poetry that came to mind where not his, but this one, by Guillaume Apollinaire: soleil cou coupé / *sun throat cut.*

Albany, May 7, 2001.

Ḥafṣa bint al-Hajj Arrakuniyya (1135- 1190):
Six Poems

Ask the lightning when it roarrips the nightcalm if it's seen my man as it makes me think of him.

By Allah, it shakes my heart & turns my eyes into a raining sky.

***

I'm jealous of my chaperone's eyes & of the time & place that claim you.

If I keep you in my eyes until the world blows up I'd still want more.

***

[Ḥafṣa called at Abu Ja'far's house & handed the porter the following poem to be given to Abu Jafar. As soon as Abu Ja'far saw the poem he said: 'This can only be Ḥafṣa.' So Abu Ja'far went to receive Ḥafṣa but she had already gone.]

The girl with the gazelle neck is here & longs to meet you.

I wonder if she'll be graced with a welcome or told you're indisposed?

***

If you were not a star I would be in the dark.

Salaam to your beauty from one who misses the thrills of your company.

***

[After Ḥafṣa had spent the night with Abu Jaʿfar in his garden, he sent her a poem telling her how pleased were the garden, the birds, the river & the breeze with the way they had spent their night. Ḥafṣa wrote back:]

When we walked along the garden path, there was no smile on the garden's face but green envy & yellow bile.

And when we stood on the riverbank, the river was not a bubble of rippling joy, & the dove cooed with spite.

You shouldn't take the world as it looks just because you're good.

Even the sky blazed on its stars to scan our love.

***

[As soon as Ḥafṣa heard of the murder of Abu Jaʿfar she wore her mourning clothes & grieved openly for him. Ḥafṣa was threatened for mourning Abu Jaʿfar & she cried out:]

They killed my love then threatened me for wearing my mourning clothes.

Let Allah bless those who grieve or untap their tears for the man killed by his haters.

Let the morning clouds, like his generous hand, shower the earth that blankets him.

translated by Abdullah al-Udhari

Ḥafṣa bint al-Ḥājj ar-Rakūniyya (c. 1135—c. 1191) was a Granadan aristocrat & one of the most celebrated Andalusian women poets of medieval Arabic literature. Her father, al-Hajj ar-Rukuni, a Berber Granadan, does not seem to have left traces among biographers, though he was probably well-off & a notable figure in the city. Around the time that the Almohads came to power in 1154, Ḥafṣa had begun a relationship with the poet Abū Jaʿfar Aḥmad ibn ʿAbd al-Malik Ibn Saʿīd. To judge from the surviving poetry, Ḥafṣa initiated the affair which continued until Abū Jaʿfar's execution in 1163. Ḥafṣa later became known as a teacher, working for Caliph Abu Yusuf Yaqub al-Mansur to educate his daughters in Marrakesh. She died there in 1190 or 1191. Around 60 lines of Ḥafṣa's poetry survive, among nineteen compositions, making Ḥafṣa the best attested of the medieval female Moorish poets (ahead of Wallada bint al-Mustakfi & Nazhun al-Garnatiya bint al-Qulai'iya). Her verse encompasses love poetry, elegy, panegyric, satirical, & even obscene verse, giving her work unusual range.

FOR GHASSAN ZAQTAN

Last week I was in Glasgow, waiting for Algerian poet Habib Tengour to arrive from Paris, as we were supposed to do a joint poetry reading and a shared presentation of *Diwan Ifrikiya* our anthology of North African Literature, at the University of Glasgow. Tengour never made it to Scotland because he never received his visa for the UK, & his passport was returned to him too late for a planned trip to Algeria for a conference. And on my first day back in the US, I am informed that Canada is refusing a visa to Palestinian poet Ghassan Zaqtan, shortlisted for the Griffin Prize together with his translator Fady Joudah. This has happened before to Zaqtan in the US: in April 2012 the US refused him a visa & he had to cancel a reading tour for the publication by Yale University Press of *Like a Straw Bird It Follows Me,* his latest volume of new & selected poems translated by Fady Joudah. (That US tour eventually happened later, after many difficulties & frustrations.) I cannot escape the feeling that right now in the Euro-American sphere anyone with an Arab name is presumed guilty & can thus be treated like a non-person.

Now, if Zaqtan was invited to Canada it is because his work is shortlisted for a major literary award, The Griffin Prize. The reason for this is the excellence of his work as a poet—though he is also a novelist, an editor & a filmmaker. With ten collections of poetry to his name, a certain consensus now suggests that he is probably the most important Palestinian poet writing today (as even Mahmoud Darwish had suggested). His is a poetry that remains, as Paul Celan said of his own historical plight, "eingedenk" ("in-thought-of," thus mindful, conscious) of the load of the past & present, even as it tries to do poetry's job, i.e. to construct, to invent, to imagine a place for an inhabitable future.

Where or how that place will be is still a predicament, Palestine being in the situation it is in right now. As I wrote in the blurb for Zaqtan's book, "the poet's trade is exile, & a Palestinian poet's trade thus a double exile: Ghassan Zaqtan's work is exemplary in that its lyrical intensity simultaneously hides & foregrounds this quest's epic dimensions." While waiting for the paranoid bureaucracies to hopefully come to their senses & allow Ghassan Zaqtan to travel to Canada, here is a poem from the book in question, as translated by Fady Joudah:

YOU'RE NOT ALONE IN THE WILDERNESS

In Jabal Najmeh, by the woods, the wizard will stop me
by a passage for boats with black masts
where the dead sit before dawn in black garments & straw masks,
a passage for the birds
where white fog swims & gates open in the brush
and where someone is talking down the slope

and bells are heard & the rustles of flapping wings

resemble the forest passing over the mountain & nicking the night!
... & peasants, fishermen & hunters, & awestruck soldiers, Moabite,
Assyrian, Kurd, Mamluk, Hebraic with claims
from Egypt, Egyptians on golden chariots, nations
from white islands, Persians with black turbans,
and idolater-philosophers bending the reeds
and Sufis seeking the root of ailment...
the flapping of wings drags the forest toward the edges of darkness!
In Jabal Najmeh, by the woods
where the absentee's prayer spreads piety's rugs
and the canyon is seen through to its limits,
the furrowed sea scent cautiously passes by
and the cracks are like a jinn's harvest
and the monks' pleas glisten
as I glimpse the ghosts of lepers sleeping on decrepit cypress

In Jabal Najmeh, by the woods,
I will hear a familiar old voice,
my father's voice throwing dice toward me

Or Malek's voice
as he tows a blond horse behind him in his elegy

Or the voice of Hussein Barghouthi
laid to rest beneath almond trees
as he instructed in the text

And my voice:
You're not alone in the wilderness!

                                              Bay Ridge, Brooklyn 29 May 2013

Fatima Mahmood:
What Was Not Conceivable

In harmony
we entered the climate of water
in harmony with the law
of the tree.
In harmony
we pronounced grass, recited hedges.
In harmony—a horizon
    of carnations.
A bundle of lavender.
    We tapped on the silence
of abandoned gardens,
walked—
the road massaging its back
with the sun's ointment
and staring at the choked
sidewalks.
The patrolman
inhabits
the first line,
sucks out the blood of language,
strips the alphabet
of its dots
and tears out
the plumes of speech.
He confiscates the states of narcissus.
He muffles
the coronets of the flowers,
buries alive the jasmine leaning out
of the gardens
of the gaze.

The fence is the noose of geography
around the waist of drowsy grass.
And time ... wilts.
In the first clarity
of an approaching poem
the boy
washes
from his chaotic face —
the dust of starved herds
led by hollowed men
to the official stable.

* * *

With staring pebbles
the beautiful children stone them,
and the math lesson embalmed
in the teacher's throat
emaciates the leap year.
The patrolman prepares
shackles
for the window
a lock
for the wind
and for the rest of eternity "invents"
an accusation
a torturer
and a scaffold.

* * *

I climb the thickets of laughter.
I return

to the branch its features
to the wind its shape
to the hedge
its pebbles.
We glare
at the frontiers of NO,
and our loud singing
flashes.
We adjust our watches
to the patrolman's
pulse rate.
Our country two embers away
was
an oven.

(...)

Translated from Arabic by Khaled Mattawa

COMMENTARY

Fatima Mahmood is an arabophone Libyan writer, & journalist. She worked as a journalist in her home country from 1976 to 1987, & then moved to Cyprus where she started a magazine (*Modern Sheherazade*) focusing on Arab women's issues, for which she served as the chief editor. She later returned to Libya but had a confrontation with, she says, the "dictatorial political regime," concerning the absence of freedom of speech. In 1995, Mahmoud was forced to seek political asylum in Germany, where she currently resides. She has one book of poems to her credit—*Ma Lam Yatauasar* or *If It's Not?* (1984)—& a new collection forthcoming.

ADONIS: FROM EXILE TO TRANSGRESSION

Poetry, that most portable & nomadic of arts, has always been the essential cultural form of the Arabic-speaking peoples. It's perfection lies in its very beginning: in the 7 (or 10) odes known as the Mu'allaqat, which predate Islam by one to two centuries. These odes, of greatly varying length, are based on the line (with caesura dividing it into two hemistichs), a number of specific—16—traditional meters & mono end-rhyme. Codified in the 8th century by al-Khalil bin Ahmad, these formal strictures changed little during the next 12 centuries, becoming an inordinately restrictive & oppressive system limiting written Arabic poetry (the various oral traditions are a different matter). Though there were a few cautious modernization attempts early in the 20th C, nothing really changed until Adonis & the generation of poets associated with *Shi'r* magazine started their three-pronged revolution in the 1950s: 1) liberation from the prison house of tradition, both in terms of thought-content & formal practice. 2) critique & re-evaluation of contemporary Arab poetry, & 3) opening up to modern foreign poetries, especially via translations. All three have been core to Adonis' poetics over fifty years of poetic practice.

At the beginning, to break the tradition, the move was towards what came to be called "prose poems," though "free verse" or "non-metrical poetry" are probably better names. Here as an example from Adonis' 1959 poem "Arwâd, Princess of Illusion…"

> Poetry burns its ancient leaves, horse-whips its routed bloodline. The future poem is a country of refusal. Ah! words of the dead! Ah! Virginity of the verb! The poem to come clothes itself in the eyelashes of childhood. It weeps & prays for the divinity of the breast.

> For whom does a timorous fire set the armpit's contours ablaze? For whom these rainy funerals of ink & nostalgia? For whom this woman purified by the wounds of the word? Oh, seashells of the island! Island of nakedness! The man tames the chest's squirrel, opens the uterus' fortress—a faceless god, earth's crown.

In hindsight, it may be easier to link this formal procedure to Saint John Perse's stanzas, than to a Max-Jacobian idea of "prose poem." Adonis needed a form of line or stanza in which Baudelairian "correspondences" could be but one of the laws of organization, & he needed a wider, more "open field" structure to accommodate the ranges of information the poet wanted to gather—from contemporary politics of Palestine & the Near East, to ancient Sumerian mythological topoi, via arguments for a cultural revolution in *Dar El Islam*, & the Sufi mystical visionary poetics of traditional masters such as Hallaj & al-Niffari, etcetera.

His first major book, *The Songs of Mihyar the Damascene* (1961) was a further breakthrough, both personally & as essential marker for the history of modern Arab poetry: it is a *book* (in the Spicerian rather than the Mallarmean sense of that word), not a haphazard gathering of lyric poems; it's overall structure is that of an ontological/metaphysical quest in seven sections or mawaqif, "stations, resting points," as I like to call them using al-Niffari's term, a term Adonis himself used to name the magazine he published in the seventies & eighties. The figure of Mihyar is that of the wandering poet, at times urban(e)-modern, at times oriental-mystic, an "I" in the poem that is not or more than a persona, that is always elsewhere—a complex occasion, just as in other poems the named figure of "Ali" represents the Arab man of today, but can also refer to Ali, the son-in-law of the Prophet, the assassinated founding figure of the Shia Islam Adonis grew up with, & is also the actual first name of the poet Adonis, Ali Ahmed Sa'id.

The poetics of *The Songs of Mihyar* are staunchly yet elegantly modernist—the formal breakthrough has been accomplished: non-metrical free-verse, longish prose-like stanzaic forms interleaved by near-gnomic lyric concretions lead to & allow the final section to be a sequence of short elegies for the great iconoclastic figures of the Arab past (the wine & boy-loving poet Abu Nuwas, the mystic & close-to-atheist Hallaj burned at the stake for his beliefs, Bashshar Ibn Burd, 8th century poet of Iranian descent whipped to death for being a free thinker), followed by longer elegies, one for "the Present Time," & one for "The First Century"—which contains the following exhortation:

> Poet, come out of the stone caves. With the mouse, the salamander and the glow-worm, come out! and bear witness for the poets who inhabit a nameless fatherland, a fatherland swollen with corpses,
>
> for the poets who read their poems to the grass.
>
> Come out and bear witness for poetry,
>
> After the candelabras comes the abyss of wings. After the sea, sudden death.
>
> ...
>
> Ecstatic under the veil of vision, enamored with refusal—man, tell us an oracle to come...

The creation of a new Arabic poetry—modern both in terms of content & form—has succeeded. In his next books, Adonis will not rest on his laurels & repeat himself: each volume will expand on the previous achievement, will travel elsewhere, push further ahead—& back, in the sense that Adonis never nihilistically rejects the past, the history of Arab (or European) poetry. His work constantly & intelligently engages with what is most alive in both traditions. If al-Khalil's canonical embalming ruined the possibilities of the classical forms for a long time, the actual poetry of the pre-Islamic period remained alive & well, & can in fact re-enter our own nomadic "extrême contemporain," as Michel Deguy calls it. Fascinating & useful, for example, the rhizomatic way in which those poems, inside their set structure, proceed with the help of independent lines, not worried about some linear coherency, true collage/montage elements, via series of images, moving from realm to realm, human—animal—vegetable—mineral, & back up, away & around & through, horizontal & vertical, taproots, transfers, without the felt need for a fixed or "organic" development. Writes Jacques Berque:

> Its most moving aspect, I mean its most mobilizing aspect, is the heteroclite richness of its calls [appels]... What is important for this process is, literally, to *transfer*. It takes the trope seriously, or at least has not yet had the time to reduce it exclusively to a rhetoric. And that rhetoric is also present in some of these poems, permitting the outrageous, the ironic and the precious to come through, as well as the reflexive from the instinctive, the factual from the originary,—it is that *dérive*, no, that perpetual hunt from realm to realm, from stadium to stadium, from genre to genre, that could appear as specifically Arabic.

And it is these aspects that Adonis will re-inscribe or, better, will allow to re-emerge in his poems, so that this most modern of poets will be ghosted by the likes of Imru' al-Qais, & if the slash he uses to punctuate a line reminds you of the breath-to-line poetics of a Charles Olson, it is also the caesura of that earliest Arab verse line.

There is a richness, a complexity in Adonis' work that ranks it among the greatest poetic achievements of the century, in any language. An *oeuvre* that is not a hasty *adequatio* of traditional Arab poetry to the ideas of the Euro-American avant-garde, but is an exploration & invention of new forms both intrinsically & extrinsically derived, based on a re-evaluation of Arabic poetics which, as he has taught us, had its Baudelaire-Rimbaldian modernist revolution under the Abbasid dynasty (750-1258 CE) with the likes of Abu Nuwas, Abu Tammam & the great mystic poets of that tradition. And yet, despite the achievement, Adonis' work is never self-satisfied, because it, or he, the poet, knows that language, even the densest, richest, most musically alive language, is not, cannot be a home, despite our desire to make it so. Language is the stranger, the other, we want to engage with & which always, & irremediably so, remains the outside. Our outside we are building a future home in, which we will never inhabit. Adonis, the poet-in-exile par excellence, knows this as his basic existential condition when he says: *"I write in a language that exiles me...If we admit the biblical & coranic story of Hagar & Ishmael, we realize that for the Arab poet, motherhood, fatherhood & language are all three born in exile. Thus, in the beginning was exile, not the word."*

This realization of exile as the initial condition of any beginning, that of poetry included, rather than making for sad-sack nostalgia, energizes the poet. To use again that originary image of the Mu'allaqat: the exile will, by chance or will, find himself faced with the atlal, the ruins of a past camp—be that Mount Thamad, or Beirut. What brought him there, & what will have to be praised after the atlal, is no longer the fast horse or camel: it is swift thought, the sharp edge of the *intelleto*, that will make sense of all the dispersals, but that itself, in order not to be autopsy scalpel having its way with a cultural corpse, will be rhythmed by melopoesis, a music that creates *tarab*—the experience of an ecstasy, reached when the musicality of the verse corresponds with the visions & thoughts expressed in the poem. For, as Rumi tells us: "If you don't experience tarab, how do you claim to be alive?"

Adonis' poetic vision, informed as it is by both past & present, is thoroughly forward-looking: for him poetry will become "the crucible in which time & space, the ancient & the modern, science & dream will meet. Poetry will concentrate always more on desire & pleasure... the poem will be transgression. And yet, like the head of Orpheus, the poem will navigate on the river Universe, completely contained in the body of language."

Fez, Morocco / Albany, NY. October/November '05

Introduction to Adonis NYC reading, 11/4/2005

Extracts from:
Conversations in the Pyrenees:
Adonis & Pierre Joris

Pierre Joris: I would like to start off by considering the text we listened to yesterday, i.e. *L'Histoire qui se déchire sur le corps d'une femme [History Torn Apart on the Body of a Woman]*. It's the title itself that immediately calls out to me. "History," is that history with a capital H? Or historical small talk of the legendary, mythopoetic kind? That's the first part of the question, the second part being how come history is ripped apart on the body—wouldn't it rather be the body that's ripped apart in history, that is ripped apart by history? Echoing yesterday evening's presentation: Hagar's exile settles the score of the feminine in all the monotheistic religions. And by following you, Adonis—"neither prophet, nor magician" —, how to open up our fields of investigation to these exilic sources, without plunging into a sedentary male / female binary? To use Nicole Peyrafitte's term, how to create an expansive, rather than an extensive space, a space that remains in question?

Adonis: Thank you, dear Pierre, for your praise, & many thanks to our hosts, & thanks also to those who are with us today. *History* here is the fate of monotheism, so it is a point of view on monotheism, but one seen from a woman's stance, from the stance of what has been rejected. The monotheistic god has only created man in his own image, not woman. As woman was not created in the image of god: she was created from a rib of man, which is why woman was originally rejected by monotheism. This vision, incarnated by the entire history of the three monotheistic religions, is what the poem tries to revise, by giving to woman a voice to criticize it radically. I don't know whether I have succeeded, or whether the poem is beautiful. But it is a critique of monotheism, as I think monotheism has to be revised, & I think, personally, i.e. this is my personal opinion, that the monotheist vision is a starting point of human beings' decadence. Strong stuff, harsh even, but that is what I believe.

PJ: So it is history with a capital H that starts off your text, not legend, even if, & we'll come back to that, it is often the effect of legend & anecdote, as covered by certain people, that then canonically turns into law. In that respect, then, I would like to ask you whether the fact that for about 95% of the poem you take a woman's voice, whether that is not an experimental form of working, *vis-à-vis* classical, or even contemporary Arabic poetry?

Adonis: Our history, ours as Arabs, is very complicated, especially with Islam. I think, first of all, we need to rethink Islam. I can't talk about Judaism, or Christianity, it's up to Jews & Christians to do that. But I can speak of Muslim monotheism. In order to better understand the poem, or better respond to your question, I must call to mind that Islam is, as you know, the last monotheism, but it was the most complete & the most closed off system, & it was above all founded on a vision of power, & thus of violence. I'd say it's been founded on three pillars. The first one being that the prophet of Islam is the so-called seal of prophethood, the last of the prophets, there will be no more prophets. So this is the first closure. The second pillar: the truths relayed by this prophet are ultimate truths, & there will by no other truths. That's the second closure. And the third: the world consists of two peoples, Muslims & non-Muslims, Jews or non-Jews, Christians or non-Christians. Essential here is therefore not the human being as human being, but the believer. The fourth pillar, if one pursues this train of thought, if one pushes it a bit further along still, is that God himself has nothing left to say, because he has said his last word to his last prophet. As far as Islam is concerned,

I would say this vision is organically related to power. And power is organically related to violence. So it is a world of power & of violence. The prophet was the messenger of God, but in practice, God has become the messenger of the prophet. He is but a means to obtain what power has on its mind. Religion, properly speaking, is but a means, an instrument, to achieve the history of power & of violence. And I think that what can be said of Islam in this respect, can also be said of Judaism & Christianity, with a small difference I'd like to point out. I make a difference between the person of Christ & the church, & when I say Christianity in this context, I'm talking about the church & not about Christ. Christ was God, who died to save man, & it was God who set woman free. He was the first. With Judaism & Islam it is, on the contrary, man who has to die to defend God. That's completely the opposite. I'll end here, with that difference.

PJ: But you weren't going to talk about other monotheistic religions. Coming myself from one, Christianity, even if I rejected it at a very young age, I'd say the Christian church is in some respects quite jealous, because Islam is, indeed, the perfection of the other monotheistic religions, & in that respect it is the most advanced point of the same thought, of the same desire for absolute power.

Adonis: Absolutely. The proof is that we're experiencing this history. Monotheism is always a beginning, & if we head into the future, what is to come is always behind us, never ahead. In all monotheisms, if one progresses, one has to go back, to Moses, to Mohammed, to Christ, the future is always the past.

PJ: So actually it is the father of all, i.e. Abraham, who is also the father of Ishmael, so the consort of Hagar who…

Adonis: I don't know, I daresay maybe one has to rethink Abraham, too. Perhaps he, too, is a pure invention, a legend, which therefore is to be rethought. But that doesn't change anything, he's there, more alive than ever, like Mohammed & like the prophets from the Bible that are still there. And it's not us, but they who rule the world today.

PJ: So the definition of the Arab nation that you give, so to speak, that you put into Hagar's mouth—"My bed, a slave nation that breeds by night & tears apart its children during the day"—can be applied to all monotheistic religions?

Adonis: Just look at a living example: Jerusalem, the sacred city for the three monotheistic religions. So if there's only one God, if the word of God is one for the three monotheisms, then that city should at least be an extraordinary example of living together, of peace, of humanity etc., whereas it is nearly the most savage city in the world—for which saving the human being is not the goal at all. Stone itself, stone is dearer to it, more human, than human beings. It doesn't defend the human, but rather an imaginary world of power, of interests, it doesn't defend the human.

PJ: Can I come back once more to something you have Hagar say: "Between me & myself, my exile, & my question about myself, remains unanswered." Why does it remain without answer, & whom does she address it to? And is she entitled to an answer from someone other than herself?

Adonis: One should always see non-subjectivity in monotheism. There is no subjectivity in a monotheistic religion like Islam. There's always the group, what we call today the *umma*. The individual is but a leaf on a tree. It doesn't have any meaning. Its meaning is to be there, on the branch of that tree, but as an individual it doesn't exist. So there's no subjectivity as such in Islam. Islam says: "If you interpret even the Quran individually, you can't do that." The interpretation of the Quran is a collective interpretation, it is the abstraction of the *umma*. So the individual, especially woman, doesn't exist. It is a word, & not a being that is master of itself & master of its destiny. And thus it doesn't exist.

PJ: So in this respect there wouldn't be a difference between women & men?

Adonis: No, one can't compare women & men. A woman is an absolute dependence, she has no independence whatsoever. None.

PJ: When you say "Woman, a tongue asleep that hasn't woken up yet. She is always…"

Adonis: It's an image to wake up women. Because I always say, that if the Arab world wants to be free, wants to free itself, it is women who have to liberate Arab men & the Arab world. If women free it, the Arab world will restore itself. Subjected, in fetters, it isn't in any case against that. So the conflict, the real war in the whole of te Arab history, is the war between the apostates & the believers. Or those who have been called apostates. It was the war between poets & the so-called doctors of law, between mysticism & orthodoxy, between philosophers & religion. And that is our history. And its richness. But unfortunately, up until now, it is forbidden to see our history from that perspective.

PJ: Hope almost arises when you again have Hagar say: "The grass is lines, / the earth a notebook, / & I am the ink of this place." & at the same time, the idea came to me that, yes, she's the ink, but there isn't yet any *kalâm*, there isn't yet a pen, that rather phallic thing if you will, that should canalize the ink. Can she become *kalâm*, too?

Adonis: It's an extraordinary thing that those who have created what we call Arab civilization were not the orthodox, the believers, the men in power, with some exceptions, there are always exceptions, but generally speaking & as far as institutions & power go, it's always been the poets that aren't believers or weren't believers, the philosophers that weren't believers, the mystics that shook up the orthodox religious vision, it's they who built this great civilization. And, for example, we absolutely do not see, in all of our poetic history, a single poet of whom we can say that he's at once a great poet & a believer, as we can say of the likes of [Paul] Claudel, for instance, or Mario Luzi. All the poets were anti-religious. And if you read from this point of view, then mysticism was a great revolution. They've changed the very conception of god.

God in mysticism isn't an exterior force that directs the world from the outside. In Islam's mysticism, too, God is not an abstract force, he's immanent, he's part of the world, of things, of trees & of mountains. And mystics have even changed the conception of identity. In Islam & the monotheistic religions, identity is: we're Christian, we're Jewish, we're Muslim. The mystic says: no, we're human, & that identity is created gradually by man. And the human being creates his identity in creating his work. So the mystics have changed everything. Even in terms of writing, so-called automatic writing, for instance, has been called an unconscious dictation. They've changed the conception of reality etc. It was a revolution inside of the Islam, but that revolution has been rejected.

(...)

Fadhila Chabbi (1946)

THE BLIND GODDESS

And the blind goddess, when we touched her
like a twinkling of the eye.
On the dry shore her hurried gait...
And in her face when sun and moon quarreled,
and in her step when the sea pecked a drop of life
the water receded—having become pregnant—for a time.
How can the letter be Seeing, Omnipotent,
a peer to the belated, jealous god.
And in the blind goddess when she dimmed
and the earth came to be
and it was the insolence of the ages.

ENGRAVING TWENTY-NINE

I left nothing behind me
No, I forgot nothing.
The words were thrown in the trash
and the expanse of whiteness.
The wolf is kind to the lamb...
That sentence I tore to shreds.
No eye-witness besides a fly rubbing its wings
beneath the autumn sun
and the heavy silver silence of a dying century,
to be born wrapped in waters of ferocity after ten meters deep
the sea snake slithers from one culture to another...

Translated from Arabic by Yaseen Noorani

COMMENTARY

Poet & novelist, Fadhila Chabbi, a cousin of Abu al-Qasim al-Shaby, was born in Tozeur, Tunisia in 1946. Professor of Arabic, she starts her career as a writer in 1988. Her first volume of poems *Odeurs de terre* stands out by its modernity of a writing refusing traditional Arabic meters. In 2000 she published *The Rise of Things*; she has been awarded a number of literary prizes. "To write," she says, " is to play with language like a god."

Introduction To Exile is my Trade: A Habib Tengour Reader

Born in 1947 in Mostaganem, Eastern Algeria, raised on the Arab & Berber voices of marketplace storytellers—see the two stories from his book *Gens de Mosta* included in this volume as an homage to his birthplace —, taken to France by his parents as a pre-adolescent, Habib Tengour has lived & worked between Algeria & Paris ever since, both incarnating and, in his writing, speaking to the nomadic & (post)-colonial condition of his countrymen & -women. Trained as an anthropologist & sociologist, Tengour has taught at universities in both countries, while emerging over the years as one of the Maghreb's most forceful & visionary francophone poetic voices of the post-colonial era. Or, as Jacqueline Arnaud, the great critique & holder of the first chair in Maghrebian studies at the University of Paris, called him: "the major author of the second generation of Algerian immigrants." The work has the desire & intelligence to be epic, or at least to invent narrative possibilities beyond the strictures of the Western / French lyric tradition, in which his colonial childhood had schooled him.

Core to it is thus the ongoing invention of a Maghrebian space for & of writing, the ongoing quest for the identification of such a space & self. For, as another Maghrebian, Jacques Derrida, put it: "Autobiographical anamnesis presupposes identification. And precisely not identity. No, an identity is never given, received or attained; only the interminable & indefinitely phantasmic process of identification endures." Or, Tengour in a kind of manifesto piece, "Maghrebian Surrealism," that situates the tradition of French Surrealism as a late local variation of a much older & wider practice:

Who is this Maghrebian? How to define him?

"The woods are white or black" despite the gone-to-earth nuances. Today definition impassions because of its implications. A domain for going astray. Political jealousy far away from the exploded sense of the true.

Indeed there does exist a divided space called the Maghreb but the Maghrebian is always elsewhere. And that is where he fulfills himself.

Jugurtha lacked money to buy Rome.

Tariq gave his name to a Spanish mountain.

Ibn Khaldun found himself obliged to hand over his steed to Tamerlane.

Abd el Krim corresponded with the Third International.

So let's take a closer look at this word: Maghreb. Usually given as the Arabic equivalent designating North Africa, i.e. the space today divided into four countries—Libya, Tunisia, Algeria & Morocco (though Mauritania should by right also be included)—it also plays in Arabic as the opposite & compliment of Mashreq, the area we call the Middle East. In this sense "Maghreb" translates as the West, the place or time of sunset—rhyming with mashreq, the place where the sun rises, the East. Indeed, the tri-consonantal root of the word is *gh-r-b*, /garaba/. From Hans Wehr's *Dictionary of Modern Written Arabic* we can gather the following cluster of meanings as offshoots of this root: "to go away, depart, absent oneself; to withdraw from, leave; to set." Now, if you do that, or are there, the meaning begins to list, like one of those ships Ulysses tries to get home on: "to be a stranger; to be strange, odd, queer, obscure, abstruse, difficult to comprehend." Which of course has consequences for the further extensions of the word's meaning—& Wehr's entry goes on: "to depart; to leave, to go westward; to expel from the homeland, banish, exile, expatriate." This logically leads to "go to a foreign country, emigrate, to be far away from one's homeland," and, obviously the farther West you go, or the more deeply you travel through it, the greater the risk to "become an occidental, become Westernized, Europeanized." All of which in due course means to "get around in the world, to see the world…" & then to "say or do a strange or amazing thing," which of course grammarians, pedants or critics may claim leads "to exceed the proper bounds, to overdo, to exaggerate," & that in turn could lead one "to laugh noisily or heartily, to guffaw." This means that exile is synonymous with West, & that to be in the west means at the same time to be in exile—wherever that West may be, in the Northern Occident or in the North African "Maghreb". So that even when you are born & live in the West=Maghreb, you are always already in the maghreb=exile.

Is it any surprise, then, that when I consulted with Habib Tengour as to a possible English title for this Reader, he immediately suggested the phrase "Exile is my trade?"

Tengour has always written in French, & is of that generation for whom French was the closest language besides the mother-tongue, i.e. spoken Algerian Arabic. Skeptical in relation to the cultural claims of post-independence Algeria—especially those that would try to impose classical Arabic as the "real" or "original" language of a country where a dialectical variation of Arabic came to overlay several strong autochthonous Berber languages & the generalized use of the colonial imposition, French—Tengour would side with the great Algerian writer Kateb Yacine when the latter claimed that Arabic was just another, older colonial imposition, & that the Algerians had every right to keep French as the victor's war booty. In "'Postcolonial' Narrative & Identity: from *Ordeal by Bow* to *Moses' Fish*," one of the essays included in this book, Tengour writes about these matters, insisting that the language question is the wrong way of addressing problems of national or personal identity:

I belong to the generation of the Tahar Djaout, Rachid Mimouni, Rabah Belrami, Abdelhamid Laghouati, Youcef Sebti, poets primarily. We did not escape the questioning about identity that tore the country apart. We dealt with it by refusing confinement inside the "false debate" around language, without however occulting the question of language. We all had learned French in school, we used it in our scriptural activities. In everyday orality, each one of us practiced his dialectical speech. I will not elaborate on this given fact, which we lived more or less badly.... French was our *spoils of war*, dearly paid for. To fall silent or to continue writing while knowing that the future would belong to the Arab language? Who could foresee the future? Nobody wanted to fall silent because identity & its narrative exceeded the imperatives of a political regime disconnected from the real. The political narrative is a discourse that veils the real; the poetical narrative is the real itself.

In the early essay "Langue, écriture et authenticité," he had already quoted Kateb Yacine on the question of the mother tongue, when he felt the need to focus more "crucially on the necessity for the writer to use the language of the people in order to touch the disinherited masses," rather than argue this language question on high cultural ground. Indeed, Kateb Yacine stopped writing in French (to devote himself to popular theater in spoken Algerian Arabic) after writing *Le polygone étoilé,* a book that ends with a reflection on the loss of the mother tongue, when Kateb the schoolboy, in love with his French school-teacher, after making quick progress in learning the colonizer's language, is asked by his mother (jealous of the foreigner's language) to teach her French too:

> Never, even on those days of success with the school teacher, did I stop feeling deep down inside me this second rupture of the umbilical cord, this internal exile that brought the schoolboy closer to his mother only to tear them away, each time a little more, from the murmur of the blood, the reproachful shivering of a language banished, in a secret agreement broken as soon as made... Thus I had lost at the same time my mother & her tongue, the only inalienable—& yet alienated—treasures!

And Tengour sees this double pull as an inevitable, inescapable dialectic, commenting that "writing, no matter the language used, is never the language 'of the mother,' but always that of the 'teacher.'" A mother tells the tale that perpetuates the oral tradition yet very soon the school—& the wider social world beyond family or even tribe, especially in a modern urban setting—will take over. Through long effective training, one's language is socialized & a new imprint made on mind & psyche. Later, of course, Tengour would argue, "the writer will have to reinvent an incantatory spontaneity from inside the servitude of the learned words." Cultural richness, literary complexity, will in fact only arise from such (and other, further) mixings, multiplications, mestizo-ings. There is no such thing as a simple identity—whatever the ideological p.r. from those in power for such is, be that in the Maghreb, in Europe or here in North America, the true *Maghreb al-aqsa*, literally, the Far West.

Thus even if the quest for an Algerian identity is all-pervasive, the man & the writing are wiser than to think that such an identity can actually be achieved once or for all—or isn't just a fiction only the heavy hand of the state wants to create in order to sedentarize the natural nomadism of man & poet. Tengour is clear about this & if returns to Algeria are inscribed in the work again & again, just as they are in the writer's life, the space invoked in the work & actually lived in, belongs to a much wider, & more shifting geography: the whole of the Mediterranean basin, the sea itself & its shores, the islands & the hinterland. For despite all the North-South p.r., the Mediterranean basin is a more culturally coherent area than first sight or first thought would permit one to believe—it would be useful in this context to reread the work of the French anthropologist, Germaine Tillion who called one of her books *Le Harem et les Cousins*, (translated as *My Cousin, My Husband*) & showed how any inhabitant of the Mediterranean *periplos*—the area she called "the republic of the Cousins," reaching from the Straights of Gibraltar to the Turkish coasts via El al-Djazā'ir, Mallorca & Marseilles, the Greek Islands & the Gulf of Tripoli—had more in common with each other than with any man or woman more than 100 miles inland—north or south of there. Though of course, Tengour will go inland, as far as he can—or at least until he meets people who can't tell an oar from a winnowing tool.

This last image, borrowed from that core text of the Mediterranean *periplos*, the Odyssey, is not chosen by chance: if any figure is central to Tengour's work, it is that of Odysseus, or Ulysses. Thus his very first book, the poetic narrative *Tapapakitaques* (a neologism in which you can hear resound immediately the father & the island of Ithaca) opens with the line (which is thus also the first line of Tengour's published opus):

My name is ULYSSES I am twenty-two I study sociology because I flunked law (p.9)

This identification continues throughout the later books—or is at least one of of the personas Tengour inhabits. Though the figure is always already double: Ulysses is the 22 year old sociology student, but also the father figure & the king of his island. In a later essay, the author will have this to say concerning the Greek hero:

Ulysses is king of Ithaca. He is the son of Laertes, the father of Telemachus, the husband of Penelope—he knows who he is, from where he comes; he keeps saying it & reminding himself of it in moments of captivity. At the same time, Ulysses is *Nobody*, which allows him to adopt all the personas necessary for his ruses in order to get out of trouble unscathed, without ever losing face, or at least that is what he believes. He divulges his name, which he states with pride & even arrogance, only once danger has been averted. His temerity induces him to brandish the signs that could identify him in front of those he loves. Yet his prudence envelops them in fictitious stories. To proceed masked, to scramble all the threads of the narrative while simultaneously desiring to be recognized immediately in all the facets of his identity, is what makes Ulysses suffer & he will be healed only by putting his "good oar" on his shoulder again, once he has overcome the ordeal of the bow.

And Jacqueline Arnaud, in her essay "Ulysse et Sindbad dans l'imaginaire maghrébin," suggests that "turned upside down, desacralized, the terms of the myth allow Tengour to broach the Algerian themes, exile, the taking of power, the role of the poet, the revolution, in a displaced manner that disrupts the generally accepted ideas." The play on this Mediterranean tale is all the more effective as the geographical reference to Ithaca as an island rhymes with the Arabic name for Algeria, al-Djazā'ir, which translates literally as "the islands."

2.

One could call Tengour's poetics a "nomadic poetics," in reference both to the/his present condition of modern nomadicity between countries & languages, & to the nomadic Beduin ancestry of his culture & the ensuing influence of pre-islamic poetry on his work, as detailed later, though one can also refer to it as an "archipelago poetics of relation" in reference to Edouard Glissant's theorizing of a (Caribbean) island poetics. At any rate, its core achievement is the successful relay between modernist Euro-American experiments & local traditions of sociopolitical & spiritual narrative explorations, or as he puts it toward the end of the "Maghrebi Surrealism" essay: "It is, finally, in Maghrebi Sufism that surrealist subversion inserts itself: 'pure psychic automatism,' '*amour fou*,' revolt, unexpected encounters, etc.... There always resides a spark of un(?) conscious Sufism in those Maghrebi writers who are not simply smart operators—go reread Kateb or Khaïr-Eddine."

Tengour's main books—besides the volumes of poetry to which we will come a bit later, the collection of short stories entitled *Gens de Mosta* (1997) & the novel *Le Poisson de Moïse* (2001)—are the prose narratives *Sultan Galiev* (1985) & *L'Epreuve de l'arc* (1990), a cycle started with *Le Vieux de la Montagne* (1983). Aware of the question of genre definition, he succeeded in side-stepping the French cartesian (and commercially motivated?) preference for calling any text that is, or looks like prose, a "roman," i.e. novel, by calling his cycle a "Relation." The choice of this term is not innocent. The French word "relation" (as does its Spanish homonym) names a genre: that of the travelogue. But this French word (and genre) is immediately ghosted by it's Arabic equivalent: the *riḥla*. A word that derives, as Stefania Pandolfo tells us, "from the verbal root *raḥla*, to set out, to depart, to move away, to emigrate, to be constantly on the go, to wander, to lead a nomadic life." The noun, meaning travel, is also the name of the genre of the travelogue, "a classical literary genre of travel writing which blossomed in Dār al-Islam, the 'land of Islam,' from the eleventh to the fifteenth century & lasted in different forms all the way to the nineteenth century." Its origins are in the diaristic writings describing an individual's hajj, or journey to Mecca, though it expanded rapidly to take in other kinds of travels, & was in fact a place of literary innovation. Pandolfo further explicates its importance:

> The riḥla as physical journey & existential displacement was the style & possibility of learning. Across the Islamic world, from one center of learning to another, a constant flow of scholars moved on endless peregrinations: from teacher to teacher, & from text to text… the imperative of traveling for seeking knowledge determined the cosmopolitan character of the centers of learning, where everyone was a foreigner & everyone belonged.

One further aspect of this genre is useful for us here:

> The riḥla is also a philosophical genre of narratives of displacement. It is a genre that might be called "cynical." As is the case of the Maqāmāt discussed by Kilito… it is a narrative genre of reflections about the journey-like character of life, the instability of fate & of the world, the irony of human existence & what Kilito names "l'identité fugitive" [fugitive identity], in the context of a "celebration of instability." (316)

Le Vieux de la Montagne, published in 1983, & the two subsequent volumes of the cycle, are a tour-de-force text that re-inscribes the genre of the *riḥla,* & its diasporic intensities, into a contemporary context of nomadic movement, both in time & place, as well as in its language & poetics. The first volume thus re-imagines through contemporary Maghrebi characters in their Occidental exile in Paris, the story of that most famous Mashreqi

Arab triumvirate of Omar Khayyam, Hassan as-Sabbah & Nizam al-Mulk. Just as Abdelwahab Meddeb breaks the transhumance (not a true nomadicity) between that "unwobbling pivot" that for so many Maghrebi writers is the Algiers/Casablanca/Tunis—Paris axis, (the umbilical cord that links the ex-colony to the old "metropole" & its language) by having his writing move through the Mashreq, i.e. the eastern parts of the Arab countries, especially Egypt & Ibn Arabi's Damascus, so Tengour re-nomadizes, re-diasporizes his work by moving through those classic loci of Arab culture in the Nippur & Baghdad of the 10th to 12th century. This is not cultural tourism, but a necessary re-appropriation to break free of the afore-mentioned axis. Nor is it a nostalgic rear-view mirror recollection of the long-gone glory of classical Arab civilization at the height of its powers. For to work with & through those specific figures, emigrating their ghosts into the fictional bodies of present-day Maghrebi in Western exile, also has to be read in terms of a poetics—or even of a poethics, to use Joan Retallack's word. If we can locate the birth of an urban, modernist Western poetics, with all the experimental & avant-guardist baggage this entails, in the late nineteenth century with Whitman in Europe & Baudelaire & Rimbaud in France (no doubt an oversimplification, but a useful shorthand), & still use those achievements as paradigmatic for our current endeavors, then, when looking at the Arab world we will have to widen our horizons beyond our chronology.

To understand not only the surface diasporicity of this endeavor, but to get to a deeper sense of the poetics—& their transformations—underlying these writings, including their genre classifications, we need a brief excursus into the history of Arabic poetics. For, as the Syrian poet Adonis has shown, just such a breakthrough had happened in urban Baghdad a millennium & more ago when poets like Abu Nuwas broke with the traditional, classical Arab poetics, whose origins go back to the pre-Islamic *Mu'allaqat* (Odes) which served as fixed & by then sterile molds—both in terms of form & content—for poetry. Claiming the past modernity of Arab poetics via those figures also claims & reclaims a non-religiously based ethics, today, in the face of a return, desired or imposed, to an puritanical Islam that would burn exactly that old/modern part of its own avant-garde heritage: the wine-drinking, boy-loving Baghdadi poets who broke the sterile molds of inherited forms & wrote the first works in which we can recognize the shapes of our own experimental modernities.

But let us take a closer look at one of Tengour's poem's from the 8oies, "Les Sandales d'Empédocle," first published in Michel Deguy's magazine *Po&sie*, & in my English translation as a chapbook from Duration Press in 1999. It presents itself *ab initio* in an astoundingly wide nomadicity: the author's name clearly locates him as an Arab, while the title refers to a Greek philosopher situated in Italy & the epigraph cites a nineteenth century German poet, Friedrich Hölderlin. There is Poundian or post-Poundian modernity visibly at work here, confirmed by the poem itself, which reads as a modernist textual montage / collage of a wide-ranging array mixing the personal & the historical. The opening lines set the tone of contemporaneity, down to the slashes used to separate the word-shards:

Traces/ Renown/ Shades/ Urns/ Life(s)/ Epoch/ Zenith/ Lucid/ Strangely/ Suspended

The 13-page text itself gives one—or at least this reader—the familiar sense of late twentieth century open-field poetics, as collaged elements move through space & time, interrupting & questioning the possibilities of the micro-narratives that develop from time to time, creating momentary pools of meditative or contemplative loci often reflecting on the act of writing itself, before dissolving as quickly as they appear. The concerns are nearly classical diasporic moves between urban centers, questions of exile, of racial identity, of the political situation in the unnamed Maghrebi country that is clearly Algeria, the matter of love under such circumstances—an urban, post-Waste Land land- & psycho-space. To this extent, Tengour's poem is a work that, besides the usual questions of tone & pitch, is rather exhilarating for a translator putting it into contemporary English. But a close reading reveals that this poem too is ghosted by the consciously worked absence/presence of a formal skeleton that links it directly to an ancient genre of Arab poetry: the ode or *qasida*.

A brief excursus is necessary here. The qasida represents the earliest extent Bedouin Arab poetry, the purest examples of which are the seven—in some canonic calculations, ten—pre-islamic Mu'allaqat, often called the "Hanging Poems" (because, embroidered on lengths of cloth, they used to be hang from the Ka'aba, the black stone in Mecca on festive occasions). They are often described as stilted, overdetermined, static poems because of their supposedly predetermined closed structures & mono-rhymes. Of greatly varying length, the odes usually start in the same place, the atlāl, or meditation on the traces of an old camp the poet comes across in his wanderings. A. Hamori, cited by Pandolfo, writes in his *The Art of Medieval Arabic Literature*:

> It can be safely said that the atlāl motif is the most dramatic among the various nasīb-themes [introductory section of the qasida]—such as the description of parting, or a dream-visit by the lady's phantom—in that it contrasts the irreversible time of human experience with the recurrences possible in nature... In the atlal scene time present has no effective contents to speak of. The past has a specific burden; the present is indeterminate except by reference to a memory. The speaker arrives at a desolate but familiar spot; we are not told what business led him

there… in this way the emptiness at the conclusion of the affair is given a depth of time… The atlāl are the point where the temporal & spatial coordinates meet.

After this introduction the poem goes on to a hymn to the poet's mount, camel or horse, (thus a moment of stasis followed by precipitous movement) after which it will often laud the poet's lady, then his weapons & exploits in the manner of the praise poem, before going on to tell of the tribe's great feats. What is fascinating, even or especially for our contemporary poetics, is the rhizomatic way in which the poem, inside that set structure, proceeds via series of images, moving from realm to realm, human—animal—vegetable—mineral, & back up, away & around & through, horizontal & vertical, taproots, transfers, without the felt need for a fixed or "organic" development. Writes Jacques Berque:

This process, where one or the other series alternate, does not worry about coherency. Its most moving aspect, I mean its most mobilizing aspect, is the heteroclite richness of its calls [appels], much more so than their respective compatibility or their mutual cohesion. What is important for this process is, literally, to *transfer*. It takes the trope seriously, or at least has not yet had the time to reduce it exclusively to a rhetoric. And that rhetoric is also present in some of these poems, permitting the outrageous, the ironic & the precious to come through, as well as the reflexive from the instinctive, the factive from the originary,—it is that *dérive*, no, that perpetual hunt from realm to realm, from stadium to stadium, from genre to genre, that could appear as specifically Arabic. [my translation]

What the poet's role can be, today in the ongoing oral tradition that still makes use of this form, or of variations thereof, is brilliantly analyzed by Stefania Pandolfo in the chapter "Impasse of the Angels" in the book of that title. In a footnote she cites Abdelfattah Kilito, who calls the poet a "melancholic archeologist"—an appellation I cannot help but link to Charles Olson's description of the poet as "archeologist of morning"—whose job is "to draw over a drawing, to write over a text half-effaced. Confronted with writing in time the poet must add something of his own for a new settlement to be born" [Pandolfo's translation].

With this in mind we can now return to Tengour's poem—& it immediately become obvious that the very title, despite its displacement into Greco-Italian areas, in itself sets the scene of an abandoned site where only ruins—the abandoned sandals—remain to speak of a past human presence. The epigraph inserted between title & poem insists again on just this situation, even if once more or further displaced by being in German. Hölderlin's lines—re-cited in French translation late in the poem itself—read:

> this country where the purple grape once loved
> to grow for a better people, & the golden fruit
> in the dark thicket, & noble wheat, & some day
> the stranger will ask, treading through the rubble
> of your temples, if this is where the city
> rose...?

Through his diasporic knowledge, the poet is able to read this poem-fragment firmly rooted in German romanticism, as another version of the classical Arabic atlal motif, the stopping (here of a stranger, not the poet) at the ruins. And as if Tengour wanted to nail this theme down, despite his wandering through other spatial-temporal realms in title & epigraph, the very first word of the poem, after the already cited slash-separated words, & given a line by itself is "Stop," modulated in the next line as "a pause of short duration," which, knowing what we know now, we can read not only as the hasty modern nomadic traveler's brief respite (in "one-night cheap hotels"), but further as the Arabic "mawqif"—a term used, among others, by the 10C Sufi poet Niffari & meaning the pause, the stop-over, the rest, the stay of the wanderer between two moments of movement, two runs, two sites, two places, two states. Abdelwahab Meddeb comments on this mawqif: "It enjoys a rest, raises itself upright; between two durations it scrutinizes briefly the instant when from its height it confronts the vision or the word exteriorizing itself." It is the space/time in which the poem will happen, where the poet can get to work. If we now turn back to those slash-separated words between epitaph & body of the text, we can read these differently too: "Traces/ Renown/ Shades/ Urns/ Life(s)/ Epoch/ Zenith/ Lucid/ Strangely/ Suspended" now reveal themselves to be not only a modernist collage of fragments but descriptions of the different sections of the poem, here adhering to the old qasida structure, here departing from it as seems necessary to the poet in order to shape that old formal ghost to his, & his world's, contemporary needs & realities.

The whole of the poem can now be read at a much more complex level than a first straight-forward reading of its surface contemporaneity allows. This analysis of one of Tengour's poems, if not applicable directly to all of the work, does however indicate the thematic & formal complexities of the writing—a complexity that not surprisingly is just as present in his prose narratives. If, as shown above, modernist collage techniques are essential in structuring the various heterogenous elements of the tengourian universe in a poem such as the "Sandal of Empedocles," then related techniques are demonstrably used in the narratives. Concerning these one could speak of an amalgam as savant as it is witty of writing drawing on oral traditions from the Maghreb transformed for contemporary writerly purposes & leavened by cinematic montage—via Tengour's fascination with, love for & knowledge of the one new 20th century art form, film. A love that is obvious in the writing itself as film often enters both as formal procedure & thematic process. Thus, if as already indicated, Odysseus is an archetypal figure of the tengourian imagination, this archetype must not be understood as a backwards pointing fixity, but as a multi-facetted cubist construction, or, better, a fluid eisensteinian montage of shimmering facets: one facet will propose the Homeric/mediterranean prototype, the next one may call on the emblematically modernist figure of the Joycean Ulysses on a pub-crawl, though a quick *fondu-enchaîné* will complicate the dance by introducing the hollywoodian antics of Kirk Douglas' Ulysses tangling with Silvana Mangano—who in a further de-doubling happens to play both Circe & Penelope in that 1953 movie that could be seen as a core event in a young Tengour's discovery of the world!

This is not the place for a lengthy critical analysis of the work, but, before closing the introduction to let Tengour's work speak for itself, I would like to briefly address the question of translation or translatability. Is this "ghost" of Arabic I have shown to haunt the French text, translatable, or better, is it necessary for the translator to try & foreground it? In the "Sandal," the poet himself has half-buried the old qasida form in his poem—as if this form itself was the ruin at which he stops, so that the "melancholic archeologist" can be seen to meditate as much on the ruins of the old form as on the questions of contemporary diasporic life. The two situations overlap, covering & enriching each other: isn't the chance discovery of an old site also the contemporary experience of today's diasporic wanderer? The poem is thus itself already a translation, i.e. a diasporic construct—Tengour's diasporic French ghosted by an old Arab nomad form, playfully deepening the absence/presence through the Greco-Italian-German layers. It seems to me that—& I believe this to be true in most cases—a translation should be as literal as possible, that is to say, it should adhere to the same absence/presence structure the poem uses. The poem's "ghost" is as invisible to the reader of the original French version as it is to the reader of the English version—unless the reader already has knowledge of those old Arabic forms. Otherwise the reader, French or English, will have to do an in-depth reading of the poem, which for any such diasporic writing means familiarizing oneself with the other's other culture. A translation should not, cannot make clearer what the original poem has purposefully hidden.

    I have approached the rest of the translations in this book in the same spirit, no matter the genre—poem or prose—of the original. Though a good part of the translation work was done during a concentrated period in the summer of 2010, the earliest attempts & versions date back some twenty years at least, given that my interest in Tengour's work goes back a very long time indeed—to the days we taught together at the University of Constantine, Algeria in the late seventies. I have had the great pleasure of being in continuous touch with the man & his work ever since & thus believe that my familiarity with the development of the *oeuvre* can only have helped the work of translation gathered here for the first time.

                                        Bay Ridge, January/February 2011.

Resources:

Jacqueline Arnaud, "Ulysse et Sindbad dans l'imaginaire maghrébin," pp. 536-553 in *L'homme méditerranéen et la mer : actes du Troisième Congrès international d'études des cultures de la Méditerranée Occidentale*, Jerba, Avril 1981 / publié par Micheline Galley et Leïla Ladjimi Sebai. Imprint Tunis : Les Editions Salammbé, c1985.

Abdelkebir Khatibi, *Love in Two Languages*, translation by Richard Howard, University of Minnesota Press 1990.

Abdelfattah Kilito, *Les séances: récits et codes culturels chez Hamadhani et Hariri*, Paris, Sindbad, 1983.

Stefania Pandolfo, "The Thin Line of Modernity in some Moroccan Debates on Subjectivity". *In* Questions of Modernity, eds. T. Mitchell & L. Abu-Lughod. The University of Minnesota Press 2000.

Ulysses (1955) Film based on Homer's Odyssey. Directed by Mario Camerini, who co-wrote the screenplay with writer Franco Brusati. With Silvana Mangano (Circe & Penelope); Kirk Douglas (Odysseus); Anthony Quinn (Antinous).

Amel Moussa (Tripoli, 1971)

A FORMAL POEM

In the old house
where my grandfather composed his formal poems
I live as a concubine in my kingdom,
my dress is wet,
and on my head I place a crown.

In the old house
where the jug is tilted
water seeps out
mixed with prayers.

In the old house
where my first cry echoed,
I spread the soil of lineage
for us to sleep on,
one soul stacked next to another.

In the old house
where my grandmother was throned a bride
I search for her shawl
and place it for my shoulders to kiss.

In the old house
I cross ancient nights
and carry fwd to dervishes.

In the old house
I hand away my embers as a dowry
to lovers bathing in rain.

In the old house
Love wears us like a cape
and the courtyard becomes
twice its size.

LOVE ME

I carry me on my fingertips.
I carry me on the galloping of my vision.
I wrap myself with a swaddling of my skin.
I embrace me, longing for myself.
I bless my flowing, my gushing.
I cradle me in my chest.
I glove these budding hands with poetry.

I claim revelation,
my engravings are on stone.
My image carries water to thirst,
and bait to fishermen's nets.
I spend the tolling of evening bells
sculpting.
I sleep in my own shade.
I wear my Bedouin nature
to spite cities.

I stroll within me
when I weary myself.
I enter a garden
that does not entice myself against me.
I love my impossible self,
the one whose feet
the earth does not know.

Translated by Khaled Mattawa

COMMENTARY

Arabophone poet Amel Moussa was born in Tripoli, Libya in 1971. Still very young, she moved to Tunis where she has lived ever since. After a thesis on *Religion in Tunisian Society* in the Sociology department of the University of Tunis, she starts writing for several Tunisian newspapers. Her first collection of poems *La femelle de l'eau* (1996) was prefaced by the writer & politician Mahmoud Messadi. Her poetry, in which Sufi influences are visible, steers a course between the sensual & the spiritual while always mindful of the exacting problems the world at large is facing. Her work has been translated into French & Italian.

On Abdelwahab Meddeb

I remember Abdelwahab Meddeb, one evening in Tangier, on the coast of that millennia-old Mediterranean that the Arab world shares with Europe. For this wise & learned man, this physician, in matters holy, who knew the illness of which Islam had to be cured, democracy was a word that held an almost religious meaning!
                    Bernard-Henri Lévy

Abdelwahab Meddeb passed away in Paris during the night from Wednesday 5 to Thursday 6 November 2014. Born in Tunis in 1946, he was among the greatest Maghrebi poets, scholars, writers & translators of his generation. Nomadic in his arts as well as in his life, he was a major traveller, magazine editor ("Dédale"), book editor (for Editions Sindbad, from 1974 to 1987, he published classics of sufism as well as many outstanding contemporary Arab authors), radio author (for 17 years he produced *Cultures d'Islam*, a weekly France Culture broadcast) & much more. Since 9/11 he had turned most of his energies towards essayistic writings focusing on modernity & Islam, interrogating what was at stake in today's civilization(s), contrasting & analyzing Occident & Orient but also ranging beyond those areas. These essays have been gathered in several volumes, only two of which are as yet available in English. His last book, *Portrait of the Poet as a Sufi*, a sequence of 155 poems, came out a few weeks before his death. I made sure to let Abdelwahab know by phone how much I treasured the copy that reached me in New York just three days before his untimely passing.

For he was also a good friend, sometime collaborator, & the man who had introduced me to the writings of Suhrawardi & Mansur al-Hallaj. We shared an intense quest for a new global poetics that would reinvent the poet's home in a nomadism whose only horizon was the world as a whole. The last time we were able to spend a few hours together was a late Friday afternoon in Paris in 2011. Over some exquisite green tea in his sunlit living room—an almost zen-like quietude enveloping us—we talked of poetry & translation, of the connection between sufi thinkings' mental & spiritual nomadic wanderings & our own *errances*. I bemoaned the fact that a few years back I had not been able to give suit to his invitation that we travel together to Damascus where he had wanted to share the Damascene traces of two figures we both held dear: the Emir Abdelkader & the sheikh al-akhbar, Ibn Arabi. Then the doorbell rang: it was a friend of his, a young Moroccan lawyer, just off the plane from Rabat where she was a member of one of the committees drafting the new constitution. She came to consult with Abdelwahab on matters of language pertaining to her committee's work. Invited to stay, I listened with great pleasure while for two hours they discussed the histories & etymologies of core words & concepts in the bilingual drafts of the constitution, dissecting & evaluating their parallel historical weight & standings in French & Arabic, reflecting on the linguistic problems this texts were throwing up. To take part in thinking through & redacting a country's new constitution: what an adventure & an honor for a poet! What a day to witness Abdelwahab Meddeb's exquisite intelligence & gift for sharing as both private poet-translator-scholar & engaged public intellectual.

But let me turn to the first time I met him in his work: sitting in the weirdly named "Hôtel Transatlantique" in El Oued, an oasis of the Souf in the North-eastern corner of the Algerian Sahara, in fall 1976, I devoured his first book, *Talismano,* sent from Paris by our publisher, Christian Bourgois. The newness of the book was instantly clear to me: no longer a novel, not a poem per se, but a autobio-narrative *cum* essay *cum* poetic perambulation of the Mediterranean North & South, it may be best to call it a *récit*, a recital—in Blanchot's sense of the *récit* as non-novel, & in reference to the concept of the "recital" as the name for the Sufi narratives. A *riḥla*, then, that immerses the reader in the meanders of the medina of Tunis, firmly setting the autobiographical origin of the author as son of a Arab scholar & denizen of one of the oldest urban centers of commerce & learning of the Maghreb. I also read that opening (which would serve me as guidebook on my next visit to Tunis two days later) as a contemporary version of the traditional opening of the classical pre-Islamic Arab ode, the *atlāl*, in which the wandering poet returns & stops at the site of an old camp. The dizzying multi-layeredness of the text is breathtaking, both formally & content-wise, as the narrative now moves, instantly, to a picnic in Venice on the tomb of Ezra Pound, from whence the text will nomadize through France, Italy & Egypt, among other places.

Talismano remains a paradigmatic text for the post-independence generation of Maghrebi writers—& is the book I recommend to any reader coming to Meddeb's work for the first time. If the cultural confrontation that formed the basis of the previous generation's novels (Kateb Yacine or Driss Chraïbi's, for ex.) is still present, there is now a more complex consciousness of the bi- or multi-lingual diasporic space that subtends the writing. Meddeb's work practices a writing commensurate with the post-colonial diasporic situation & one that takes into account both the oral & the scriptural aspects of the Arabic language that ghosts the French text. For here, & maybe for the first time, Arabic ghosts the text not as some originary but lost mother-tongue become unavailable in order to prove or help achieve the post-colonial modernity of the author through its overt rejection. Nor is it a *Verfremdungseffekt* or an orientalizing ornament or realistic anchoring of the place, as is the case in more naively representational novels. The Arabic language's absence-presence works as a consciously thought through & acknowledged relationship to the *other* language, as witness, worker, energizer, transformer of the diasporic language. The writing is thus a *textum*, a weaving of the visible thread of the French & the invisible thread of Arabic—& it is the interweaving of both in a conscious & active engagement with the two languages that creates the final work, a true *amour bi-lingue*, or bi-lingual love, to use Abdelkebir Khatibi's phrase. This deep bi-cultural love unites the intellectual enlightenment he so cherished in the Occidental tradition with that other shining light of his moral stance as expressed by his master Ibn Arabi in these words: "I believe in the religion of love, whatever direction its caravans may take—for love is my religion & faith."

But Arabic is not only another language at the levels of vocabulary, grammar, syntax, etcetera. It is also other in its scripturality, through which it connects to a core Arab art, calligraphy, involving both work on & extension of the act of writing, & which both obeys & circumvents the Qur'anic proscription of the representational. Here is how Meddeb himself formulates his position: "How then should he write who to begin with calligraphs, then works (in) this language which fascinates, to begin with, because mistress of what seems a chimerical power?" Meddeb speaks of this kind of work as "allography"—a writing that retools French not by simply allowing Arabic words in, but by refiguring it at the grammatical & syntactical level (something that the reader experiences very strongly as a violence done to the language, especially as French is one of the most recalcitrant languages when it comes to such wrenchings—but that also presents a range of difficulties for the translator). Work such as Meddeb's seems to me to be much more boundary-breaking & challenging than most of the "metropolitan" French so-called avant-garde writing.

My friend, stuck as I am in the farthest West (my American Maghreb), I could only accompany you in heart & mind on your final journey home to the place of your birth. Like Sohrawardi, the great Sufi sage, you have finally returned from your "Occidental exile," as in your book of that title, where you wrote: "Disaster leads from darkness to light, from night to dawn, from the Occident to the Orient." May the light your life's work has generated continue to shine & help dispel the darknesses that are endangering both our worlds, our Occident & our Orient.

Mbarka Mint al-Barra'

POETRY & I

   The sin is that I wasn't a stone
     & the troubles of the world make me sleepless
And I shield myself with poetry
     & it keeps me company when I'm far from home
And poetry is my satchel that I will always carry with me
     It holds the taste & fragrance of the earth
It holds thickets of prickly branches
     It holds palm fronds loaded with dates
It paints all the stories of love in my language
     Its colors form the spectrum from grape to dawn
And I said bring the most beautiful of stringed instruments
     So the universe may know how music flows
And play its soothing melody
     That brings justice to those who are in love
Letters burden this world of mine
     Trouble leeches ink from the quill
Trouble leeches ink from the quill
     When I read of the longing of lovers I burn

   The literal translation of this poem was made by Joel Mitchell
   The final translated version of the poem is by *The Poetry Translation Workshop*

COMMENTARY

Mbarka Mint al-Barra' is a Mauritanian poet & teacher writing primarily in Arabic. She is very active in the cultural & literary life of her country, & has achieved some renown elsewhere in the Arab world. She frequently takes part in literary festivals in other Arab countries. In the "country of the million poets," as Mauritania is often called, al-Barra belongs to the third generation of poets. Like many of this group, she resorted to the use of dialogue in her poems & a narrative style to address the realities of Mauritanian society & uses free verse in some of her poems. She borrows images from religious texts, ancient Arab history & classical Arabic texts to portray conditions in her country. The symbolism of the religious stories is particularly effective in a country deeply rooted in Arab-Islamic traditions. Al-Barra uses both free verse & rhymed poetry, borrowing images from her own environment, which explains the frequent use of palm trees & sand. (via *The Poetry Translation Workshop*)

Homage to Mohammed Bennis: "A Shared Testament"

> *hal ghadara al-shu'ara'u min mutarradame*
> *am hal 'arafta-l-dara ba'da tawahhumi*
>
> Antar
>
> *Have the poets left a single spot for a patch to be sewn?*
> *Or did you recognize the abode after long meditation?*
> trad. Arberry
>
> *Me laissent-ils, les poètes, quelque chose*
> *à empiécer*
> *ou est-ce qu'après l'illusion*
> *je reconnaîtrais la demeure?*
> trad. Jacques Berque

In 2008 in Tangiers, Mohammed Bennis inscribed a copy of his book *Le Livre de l'amour* to me thus: "Pour Pierre Joris / dans / LE LIVRE DE L'AMOUR **un testament en partage**." I will try to address these two core-vortexes of poetry—the *testamentary* & the *sharing*—but first let me say the pleasure & honor it is to be here today & to be part of this homage to an immense poet, a poet not only of Morocco, of the Maghreb, not only of the Maghreb & the Mashreq, but of the world. World-poet, then.

Though, that concept—world-poet—is a rhetorical oversimplification: we live, have to live, especially today, in more than just one world, because there are many worlds, & it behooves the poet to be aware of this multiplicity. The American poet Robert Duncan even applied this thought to the universe—writing, that we live in a **multiverse** & that our poetry has to be true to this fact. And Mohammed Bennis indeed does this in his writing &

thinking. As he said, when asked how he deals & if he thinks he has to choose between his Arab & his Franco-Occidental worlds: "I do not mark a difference between the two worlds. From the beginning on, it was clear to me that I needed to understand the two worlds, as they have their traces on my body. The problem is not to choose between the two worlds, but how to be free in relation, vis-a-vis, yourself & the other." His choice is what I have elsewhere called a nomad's choice: the ability (and the power) to move, & keep moving, between these worlds as needed for the creation of a life in poetry & a poetry in life that be true to both sides—& even to more than two sides, because, it seems to me that today one of the essential moves is to go beyond the dualism of dialectic thinking, be it Occident-Orient, North-South, good-evil, pure-impure, or however it is framed. The essential paradox & truth is this: *one world means many*. And, to use a word by the German poet Hölderlin, Mohammed Bennis is "eingedenk" of this fact, it is inscribed in both his life & his writings. This word, "eingedenk," links both to "Gedanken," i.e. thought, thinking, & to "danken," to thank & to be thankful, if we wanted to think with Heidegger. In my English, the word means to be **mindful**, to be conscious of the events of both present & past—& to have the future too in mind. An ecology of time, so to speak. And thus we are, immediately in the "*testament*," the testamentary, because the poet's job is indeed to "bear witness," to stand as witness to & to transmit the culture he or she comes from—for Bennis this means the whole of Arab poetics—& the one or the ones one has investigated, in his case specifically French culture.

Two examples will show this: From the modern Arabic tradition in the first part of the 20C century comes the figure of Badr Shakir Al-Sayyab of whom Bennis writes: "his poetry gave me the freedom to know the meaning of the presence of death in my life." & from the other tradition Bennis has investigated comes the figure of Stéphane Mallarmé, the great late 19C French avant-garde poet. If the modern Arabic tradition from Ali Ahamad Bakathir

& al-Sayyab to Adonis looked back for the renewal of the forms of Arab poetry primarily to the great Occidental modernists from Baudelaire to T.S. Eliot to create formal possibilities in terms of "free verse (shi'r hurr)" & the prose poem, it neglected the even more profound & deeply disruptive (in both linguistic & intellectual) terms poetry of Mallarmé. But, as Bennis has stated: "As a modern Arab poet, I am committed to French culture & its modernity. The French language was the home of a poetic revolution & it gave my Arabic language a poetic strength, more valuable than any of the other modern languages." The testamentary quality of Mohammed Bennis' magisterial, magnificent translation of *Un coup de dé jamais n'abolira le hasard* cannot be overlooked, in fact this work & its material production as collaboratively created by Bennis, Bernard Noël & Isabella Checcaglini, realizes a vertiginously impossible feat: a translation that is more accurate than the original, both bringing the first Arabic translation of this masterwork to the Maghreb & the Mashreq, & in the same movement, giving back to the Occident from which the poem came, its first actually accurate version of that poem, as it had never been presented there the way Mallarmé had intended the poem to be. This marks a profound & unique occasion: how the passage from one culture to the other by translation can & does discover & restore the original work for the first time, more than a century after its conception. An act that further opens up a whole range of new formal possibilities for the reader of the translation & thus for Arabic poetry. It also enables us, Occidentals, to start reading the oeuvre of Mohammed Bennis from another, a wider angle, as, for example Camilo Gomez-Rivas understands when he writes: "The semantic shifts one encounters in a single line of poetry by Mohammed Bennis can be startling. Words one had thought to know well appear dissociated from their common senses, taking on unexpected shades of meaning. Even their shapes on the page are plastic, three dimensional. Freed from the usual points of reference, stripped of worn metaphors, the words appear to act of their own volition, with abilities outside traditional usage or grammatical functions."

As Bennis himself notes in his superb "Journal of a translation," which accompanies the Ypsilon edition—a journal which, my dear Mohammed, I am presently in the process of translating into English, a language realm of poetics where it is much needed—(& I quote:) " To write & to translate are two mirror actions of my poetic practice. The one brings its lack to the other. And in this lack I continue to sense the vibration of a hidden or nowhere to be found word." & a bit further on, linking this modern testamentary to an older one, that of al-Andalus, he says:

> [A throw of the dice] is also [an exception in modern poetry] for me, a descendant from a poetic tradition that wants to 'purify the words of the tribe.' Without this poem, the modernity of Arabic poetry will remain far, very far away from a space where the poem can make a new beginning for both thought & form. *A Throw of the Dice* reminds me in a different manner of the so overlooked experience of space in the poetry of al-Andalus. An Other Space, because toward the 12c the notion of space had entered Anda-lusian poetry while tradition had privileged the voice, that is to say, *time.*

And so Bennis, in one fell swoop, brings together the oldest & the newest traditions, joins Orient & Occident, & in the process creates a new, open possibility for Arabic poetry—but not only for Arabic poetry, for all poetry, because it behooves us poets of the Occident to go & learn & draw from this masterly achievement.

Let me further address that most loving testamentary work of Bennis, *Le livre de l'amour,* in which he writes through & brings into the light of day—of today—in the process rendering this light ecstatic once again—the work of Ibn Hazm, the great master from 11C al-Andalus, & his book, the *Ring of the Dove*. Here the epigraph, a poem attributed to an anonymous pre-islamic beduin woman: "Hidden so as not to be seen / Apparent so as not to be hidden / It is latent / like the fire in the stone / is kindled by rubbing / disappears if neglected / If it is not a twig of madness / it is the quintessence of magic." A woman poet is set at the head of the book: someday someone will have to write a long essay on the role of women in Bennis's poetry—it seems to me that his stance here is as revolutionary as are his formal advances.

Let me turn to our second term: *le partage*, the sharing—& let me give it here, in this oral presentation, another name, namely in arabic, *ziyafah*, hospitality. A hospitality that, just like the testamentary, is acted out both in the work & the life. Permit me to remember the first occasion, shortly after our first meeting at a poetry festival in Rabat, on which Mohammed Bennis invited me & Jerome & Diane Rothenberg to his house in Mohammedia. The pleasure of all of us around a table, of meeting Oomama, & the sharing of superb food & talk, from news of poetry there in the Maghreb to what was happening elsewhere in the world, in the Far West, the Far Maghreb of the U.S., as Jerome & I had tried to outline it in our anthologies, to talk about Rothenberg's retrievals of ancient oral poetries & the local situation of Amazigh poetries. It is such *ziyafah* that leads to community, to the making of community, perhaps the highest achievement poetry is capable of—we know that other worldly rewards do not apply.

I happily proffered Mohammed Bennis *ziyafah* in return when he came to New York in April 2011—on which occasion he was also able, as the invited poet-scholar, to appraise an attentive New York audience of the situation & the advances of Arabic poetry, in the context of the Poets' House series, *Illuminated Verses: Poetries of the Islamic World*. On that day, as is the custom, our dialogue was followed by a reading—extracts of which are still available online. I think the reading itself, the absolute clarity & rhythmic perfection of the poems, coupled with the sheer beauty of the Arabic language as enunciated by Bennis, convinced even those in the audience who had never heard Arabic, that this was a language made for poetry, maybe more than most. In return, New York itself offered us its hospitality as on that day & the next we walked & talked through the ever so welcoming city, listening to some of the 800 languages spoken there, taking in the architecture & all that makes New York New York. *Ziyafah*, indeed, on that most basic & material—& yet already profoundly cultural—level. Yet, we can take it further, theorize it more deeply. Permit me to draw on another great nomadic poet, Michel Deguy, who writes, with *The Energy of Despair*—the title of an essay of his—& a deep desire for a "poetics continued by any means available," meant to help us locate the place & circumstance we (hope to) come to after a long day of moving, of nomadic wandering in the word & in space: "The principle of poetry is the principle of hospitality. Poetry is the host (of the poem) of the circumstance. What is this circumstance? Such perhaps is the essence of the host: one doesn't know *who* it is. The host is always unknown; without identity." For that is the movement of the real poem, it's non-identity with author or subject, & yet its circumstance of community-making, even if the community turns out to be, in George Bataille's terms, "the community of those who have no community."

And yet, if hospitality has to be total—see Jacques Derrida's, that Maghrebi wanderer's, errancy-writings around the hostis/hospes theme—hospitality can, & has also to be critical, especially when it comes to welcoming objects & images into our work—& finding the accurate place for them around the festive table of the poem. It is exactly here that Mohammed Bennis shows himself as a highly demanding because visionary poet. When cities & rivers & people enter his poetry they do not do so as either hypertrophied romantic *topoi*, or metaphors for bloated, vague, "poetic" feelings, no, to enter the tent, the *bayt*, of the poem & be given hospitality in the book, they have to reveal their depth, their honest mettle, their visionary potential. Bernard Noël has maybe best described this process when he writes that in a Bennis poem "one couldn't stop to slide from a fact to its volatilization, which results in a reinforcement of strangeness, if a minimum of representation didn't permit—if I dare say so—to have started with feet firmly planted." & further: "There is in Bennis' manner of breaking down the visible, and thus its heaviness, a sort of mythographic ferment that makes of him an abstractor of images; he pressurizes them violently, rather than unfolding them in order to bedazzle." This lends Bennis' work, Noël again, "a rigor that refuses all concessions to a reductive lyricism & to those decorative digressions so frequent in poetry." And it seems to me that here is where our Mallarmean poet (i.e. a poet of space) also relies on, listens to, his heritage, the testamentary of his culture, namely the sound of Arabic, here the words are sounded to be proved accurate to the poem underhand. This is however not a present space being checked by a past time, but two presents presenting themselves, reticulating so as to create the strong open, breath-probed & -proven web of the poem.

Let me also here, now, in his presence, express my deep gratitude for another occasion of Mohammed Bennis' *ziyafah*—his hospitality toward my own nomadic attempts to enter poetically, to take part in & share, the world of Sufi poets & mystics, from Mansour al-Hallaj & Niffari to al-sheikh al-akhbar, Ibn Arabi. In a superb essay he was kind enough to explain & diffuse my own confusions concerning the matters of the mawaqif, the stations, that have been important concepts in my elaboration of a contemporary nomad poetics over the last twenty-five or so years. If I came to these matters first via my own readings in Henry Corbin (especially the latter's notion of "ta'wil"—very important for a number of us Occidental poets, but that's a matter for another day) & Louis Massignon, it was the friendship with Abdelwahab Meddeb that fired my imagination in the late seventies. Now, with our common friend gone, I will have to—& do so with great confidence & ease—rely on Mohammed Bennis to keep me on the right path on these matters.

Finally, I would like to say that what we need right now in North America & the rest of the anglophone world, & what I am militating for, is a large translated collection, a "reader" as we say, of Mohammed Bennis' work, including not only the core poetry, but also a range of his essays—even if unhappily we probably can't for some time have his 4-volume critical work on Modern Arab Poetry, *Structure & Transmutations*. Given the multiverse we live in, given its dangers & perils, given the political & religious diktats our world is yoked to, it is essential that visionary work that labors at giving precedence to eros (love) over nike (strife)—to use the distinctions the Greek philosopher Empedocles proposed—which is the poet's task, be honored, read, translated. Thank you, Mohammed Bennis, for your *leaves of splendor*.

Aïcha Mint Chighaly (Kaédi 1962)

PRAISE ON THE SITE OF AFTOUT

O my beloved, remember the past,
Your flowing tears (full of) nostalgia
At the sight of Dagreg and Toueijilatt
From the height of Lahrach
There next to the wells.
And there, the place called Limé
The delightful backwater of Weymé Bameyré
Just a short morning (walk) away.
Before you get there, is the Kedan pass.
And over there a little further on,
The ould Moilid gully.
Before that you see many trees & clearings.
And there is Djeb, silhouetted against the West.
O my beloved, do not let yourself be led
Into a dead-end, for to the east are the cliffs.
That was the domain of the Moors.
In these places, there is no longer music lovers
Nor caravans passing alongside herds of deer.
There is no other divinity but God.

NOSTALGIC SONG ABOUT LIFE

Oh! These are uncertain times.
Even one moment of pleasure
Is sure to be followed by days of pain.
Today I went past the old camp ground
And I saw the baobab branch which used to
stand behind the tents.
This baobab branch was burned all black.

Oh! Such sadness & desolation.
The one who burned that branch is ignorant.
There is no other divinity but God.
O my beloved, speak.
Because I am too shy, I cannot
Come see you at your parents house.
And you, you did not take the precaution of leaving
and going away
So that I could find you.

> French translation of the poems,
> SHEIKH MOHAMMED EL-ARBI
> (English translation, J. Crews)

COMMENTARY

(1)   Born in 1962 in Kaédi, Aïcha Mint Chighaly is the daughter of Yuba al-Mokhtar ould Chighaly, one of the best-known griots of the past century. The Chighaly family comes from the border area with Senegal, but moved to Nouakchott in 1982. Aïcha owes her reputation in her own country to her abilities as a singer & player of the *ardin* harp, but also to the family heritage in music & poetry. She is always accompanied by her band, made up of her brothers & her sister-in-law, who all studied with her father. She launched her international career in 1996 with her first CD for the *Maison des Cultures du Monde* in Paris & since then has toured many countries in Europe, Africa, the Gulf & also Japan.

(2)   The music of the griots of Mauritania is called *Azawan*, & is a very scholarly art, following strict theory & played by professional musicians with a long & specialist training. The songs are accompanied by three instruments: the *ardin* harp, played by Aïcha, is a women's instrument made of a half-calabash & has eleven or fourteen strings; the *tidnit*, a four-stringed lute played exclusively by men; & the *tbal* kettledrum, a hemispherical drum made from a hollowed-out piece of wood, which can reach 1 m in diameter.

Prize Fights

September & October are known in Paris as 'la rentrée', which the dictionary gives as 'the beginning of term' & 'return to the stage, reappearance (of actor after absence)'. Both these meanings apply: while the young ones are bundled off to school, the curtain rises on the many actors, stage managers & prompters of the literary scene. A hundred or so novels come out at roughly the same time, flanked by a vast array of essays, biographies, philosophical treaties, etc. It is a weird kind of carnival that reaches its climax in late November when ten writers, the prestigious jury of the Prix Goncourt, meet at their traditional watering hole, the Restaurant Druou to announce the winner of France's most coveted literary award. The prize has little to do with literary merit these days; it is barely more than an infight - for large financial stakes - between the major Paris publishers. Bernard Clavel, who got the prize in 1968, was elected to the Goncourt jury in1971, & has resigned in disgust since then. He writes in *Le Monde:* 'The truth is that only three publishers of novels are actually represented out of a total of over thirty ... Chances for the winner to be a writer not published by Gallimard, Le Seuil or Grasset are practically nil. I don't know for sure if the whole thing is rigged. but if that word is too shocking, let's find another one.'

On 19 November the result of the 1979 Prix Goncourt was announced: it went to Antonine Maillet for her novel *Pelagie-la-Charette*, published by ... Grasset. The same day, in the same restaurant, the judges of the Prix Renaudot—set up originally to counter the Goncourt—announced their choice: Jean-Marc Robert's novel *Affaires Etrangeres*, published by ... Le Seuil. Any Paris publisher is pleased & satisfied when a good novel sells 10,000 copies, but a novel that gets the Goncourt will sell between 250,000 & a million copies, which is, of course, what the whole struggle was about.

So much for the more public & venal aspects of 'la rentrée'. Among the many novels published this autumn there is at least one that should be mentioned here. Its author is not French—although he writes in French—but Algerian. His name is Rachid Boudjedra; this, his fifth novel, is called *The 1001 Years of Nostalgia* & is published by Denoel. It is a measure of the latent racism & overt ethnocentricity of the ex-colonial masters that a novel as powerful as this one doesn't stand a snowball's chance in hell—or in the Sahara—of getting one of the major autumn prizes. But to the matter of the book: somewhere on the edge of the great desert there is a village called Manama, 'built on the crumbling strata of oblivion, immured in the shelter of the bulwarks of the ancestral order'. Worn threadbare by the unrelenting aggression of time & the desert, the ancestral order is losing its grip on the communal psyche, leaving it wide open to the random raiding incursions of the modern & the foreign. The harshness of life is warded off with ancient & modern magic—so much so that no one knows any longer how to untangle the threads of what is real & what is dream. Boudjedra's near-hallucinatory prose, his long wave-like sentences that never permit the security of knowing in advance where they will deposit the dazzled reader, reinforce this oneiric mood. A dream-like topos, but far from unreal: the author's love for accurately named particulars, the detailed investigation of social & familiar ties, of the minutiae of daily life, all these combine to keep Manama from slipping into fantasy. The time sequences of the ancestral order—cyclical & repetitive—are jolted, shot through & reshaped by the barbed arrows of a more linear, more modern time. It is the interplay of these two orders that gives the novel tension as well as structural integrity. Its main concern is neatly foreshadowed in the protagonist's name: SNP Mohamed. SNP means 'Sans Nom Patronymique', 'Without a Surname': a common colonial practice used to undermine any sense of identity the 'native' might have or want to hold on to. This quest for a viable identity taking into account the old & the new order is carried on in the midst of an epic power struggle pitching the hero's family & the villagers against the pompous greedy local dictator. The truly Rabelaisian threads of the story are woven into a tapestry which leaves the reader with the sense of having met a world quite alien to his own, while forcing him to wonder exactly how solid, how real his own world, & his assumptions about it, are. Given the West's current fascination with things Arabic & Islamic, it is surprising that no British or American publisher has deemed worthwhile to make this or his first novel, *La Repudiation* available to the English-peaking public. The latter provides what must certainly be the most powerful account of the sexual workings inside the Islamic family structure in contemporary North Africa. It is, incidentally, one novel by Boudjedra still banned in puritanical Algeria, where the author has recently returned, after years of exile in France.

September also saw the return of Vaneigem. A main figure of French politics in the Sixties (his 1967 book *Traité du Savoir-Vivre a l'Usage des Jeunes Générations* - published in England as *The Revolution of Everyday Life* by Practical Paradise Publications - was a seminal text analyzing the various subjective aspects of alienation), Vaneigem left the Situationist International in 1970, & not much was heard from him since then. Now he's back with *The Book of Pleasures* (Encre Editions) just in time to celebrate the end of the grim & sad Seventies. His main concerns are still those of the *Traité*, but it is refreshing to find someone thinking clearly outside the two crippling sets of hypotheses that have cornered the ideological world market. Economic imperialism is the basis for repressive political systems, socialist as well as capitalist. 'The fragmentation that exchange value imposes on living tolerates only . . . embryos patiently dried in the social test-tube of rentability, beings condemned never to belong to themselves because they belong to a power stripped first of its divine mantle & then of its ideological meat, reveals the skeletal mechanism of its abstraction: the economy.' Against this he pitches desire as being 'irreducible to economy', & pleasure as the touchstone from which to 'fight the universal proletarisation of the body'. Only the autonomous emancipation of the individual can lead to a classless society. The basis of a self-managing society, this self-regulating individual is a man or woman who has radically extirpated his or her addictive need for power & dominance - economic, sexual, political - by showing it up for the entropic, death-oriented economy it is. Vaneigem knows the dangers of this stance, but concludes by saying: 'I prefer a spontaneous error to an imposed truth. Rather the creator's stumblings than the leader's coherence.' A refreshing & stimulating book.

Zahra el Hasnaui Ahmed

VOICES

To all the Sahrawi voices locked in graves and jails;
those voices that, nevertheless, bring down more than walls.

Perhaps you think your voice does not reach me,
that the evil sirocco carries it off
before it fills my senses.
Perhaps you dream that the echo is mute
the mirror blind and your lines
cowardice.
Your clones pile up,
and in a riot they fight
in black and white
to leave my throat.
Sometimes I spit,
almost always I gobble
down wrath and blood,
and peace and dirt.
I would like to chain
your hands to mine
and swing open the roof
top up to the stars.
I would like to wash
the anger from your eyes.
Thirty voices,
thirty times
repeat the history,
because no one or thing,
ever could or can tame
the voices that brush
against the soul.

GAZES

Dedicated to Fatimetu. This friend had to inform her mother, one morning, that her fourth brother had died in battle. The evidently shocking answer of her mother, "prepare breakfast and send the kids to school," I understood once she added, "let us not allow him to have died in vain."

Grey dawn, dyed red, forebodes the worst.
You shoot an inquisitive look, understanding, accepting,
Gash in the heart, serene expression.
Your orphan tear contrasts my downpour
Of pain, your calm against my blustery awakening.
My eyes exclaim: Scream! Cry! Pull out this merciless
Spear launched by ignorant ambition.
Your relatives take me in, consoling, comforting.
Like a craftsman fearful of fragile work, you breath in, fold up and,
With obstinate parsimony, cherish his scanty belongings in your trunk.
Get up, you whisper, the sun has already risen.

COMMENTARY

Zahra El Hasnaui Ahmed was born in El Aaiún, the capital of the old Spanish Sahara. After the Moroccan invasion, she first went to study a thousand kilometers away from El Aaiún, & then to Madrid where she received her degree in English Philology at the Universidad Complutense. She returned to the Sahara, living in the refugee camps of Tindouf, where for several years she collaborated on Spanish language programs for National Sahrawi Radio. She currently resides in Spain & has contributed to several Sahrawi poetry anthologies, including *Aaiún, gritando lo que se siente* (2006), *Um Draiga* (2007) & 31. *Treinta y uno*, *Thirty one* (2007).

Translation from Spanish & commentary by Joseph Mulligan

On Nabile Farès

1) **Introduction to Nabile Farès'** *A Passenger from the West.*

It was one of those uncomfortable clammy-wet nasty freezing winter days the city of Constantine uses it would seem ironically (though it could as well be with or from a total lack of irony) to remind you (if you have been there for more than one season— whoever you may or may not be) to remind you, I said, of that breath-taking & -burning uncomfortably dry & hot—slightly above 40 degree Celsius!—summer day you (you: same as above) claimed as the worst day of the season upon your arrival in this city (Constantine, Algeria) so perilously pitched on a rock outcropping above the high plains, a spur—if not necessarily beauty (though that too can be perceived eventually, if you're patient enough)—in the eye of the beholder.

A sentence (the previous one) that, I would like to believe, sort of wrote itself already—mimetic homage, I hope—toward the writing of Nabile Farès, before I (the you of the previous one) could even get around to mentioning him, as if it (the sentence) knew better than I where so much of the pleasure in reading his (Farès') work lies, namely—no, not in the names, but in the process of the sentence itself—in the nomadicity or transhumancy (again the process, not the noun : which is why the spell-checker claims both those words, nomadicity, transhumancy, as grammatically incorrect) of the language, the thinking, the action, i.e. in what happens at any given moment all over the place—if you let it.

Okay. *Bon.* Back to Constantine, circa (a word which reminds me that the city's old Phoenician name was Cirta, meaning "city carved into rock") early 1977, a nasty day, fire in a kanoun & homemade pastis not to *keep* but to try to *get* warm, in my post-colonial coopérant flat in the quarter of Oued el-Had, on the homemade (by a previous coopérant) sofa under two sheep skins & a Berber blanket, reading Nabile Farès' *Un passager de l'Occident*. We got there, we finally got to the book in hand—though the one you're holding is of course the first English translation of *Un passager*, coming out 39 years after its original publication. Thus 32 years after I first read it —on which occasion, I remember, I kept turning back every so often to the front cover to ponder the word printed there under the larger black title in small red caps, namely (& here it is indeed a noun) the word "roman." It was the way the French publishing house, *Editions du Seuil*, announced its color (literal translation of "annoncer la couleur:" to honestly & straightforwardly say something) in terms of genre. This was, they claimed, a "roman," a "novel" (I'll leave quotation marks around the English word too) thus supposedly a work of "fiction," & the reason I kept going back to the cover was because 1) that was a puzzling description of what I was reading, & 2) it was also a renewable source of mirth to think that the French tried to sell this burning truth-telling as a piece of fiction.

("Editions du Seuil" means literally "Publications of the Threshold" & indeed in those days it was literally the only major Paris publisher who carried the young writers from the newly independent Maghreb who were still—& forever—wedded to the French language across the public threshold of the French capital, even if they there was always a chance that an author could be dropped indecorously if economic or ideological reason demanded it. Still, Seuil was doing a job no publisher in the newly independent but politically & culturally sternly policed country was allowed to do or would dare take on.)

So, no: what you are about to start to read (unless you already have, & , as many, me included, do, read intros last, the way they are written & should be read) is not a "novel," in any customary sense. Novels are mimetic bourgeois leisure art while this is writing whose intensity & self-consciousness in relation to its language matter & its existential urgency is closer to the white heat of poetry, & is an enactment & not a mere representation of something, a life, or a fact, say, historical or mental of that life. Thus, the opening section is a "true to life" account of the author's meeting with James Baldwin for an interview published in *Jeune Afrique*, the major political/cultural third world magazine of the period (an English translation of the actual interview has been added to this translation of the "novel.") This meeting happened—but, more importantly, keeps happening in this writing, exhilaratingly, creating that meridian—as Paul Celan might have said—that connects the Algerian writer's Maghreb to the African American writer's America through the node of Paris.

Now turn the page & you're in a nightclub in Paris, & soon the author (for he is the "I" of the tale, no need & no time to invent some novelistic persona) will embark with his beloved Conchita for an amorous stay in Northern Spain, which of course comes to an end & not so "of course-ly" the narrative migrates toward the tale of Ali-Saïd's short life in colonial Algeria & now the meridians bend outwards, become tangents & fly off into the cosmo-mythopoetic with a final section rooted in Berber folktales that twist into spiraling dialogues between earth & the setting sun. When you close the book, you may want to catch your breath—for a few moments before the desire to start the ride all over again overwhelms you. Don't resist, give into it! Read it again! It will be a different book, an even richer book, just as it was a different & richer book rereading it now here in New York from when I read it way back then in Oued el-Had, Constantine.

It is also good to know that this book has finally been translated—& excellently so—& is thus available to an English-speaking public, just as Farès' books are starting to be republished (or rather: published for the first time) by an Algerian publisher & are thus also made available to a new generation of Algerian readers. Maybe the energy created by these occasions will translate in further translations of Farès oeuvre: we need what he has to say to make sense of the complexity of this, our, world in all its beautiful & terrifying disorder.

Bay Ridge, 7 February 2010

2) Breakfast with Nabil Farès' Bikini

Sitting in a café not 2 blocks away from where the book was written—at least partially, at least if we believe the author, I read (& reread, rereread—*ri,ri,ri*, laughing laughter spreads ((like the wind—rhi, in Arabic—?)) like something on my breakfast bread) Nabile Farès' *Le Champ des Oliviers* ("The Olive Grove"), book 1 of his *La Découverte Du Nouveau Monde*, "The Disvovery of the New World"—which, do I have to add, is NOT about America, but about Algeria, its invention, or re-invention.

When I read I translate (we all do that, though mainly into "sense," our sense, taking it away from language) but I am afflicted: I (also) translate as I read into other languages, into English in this case as the original text is in French (well, at least on the surface: it is traversed by Kabyle Berber & Arabic, or those are it's basement vaults, its subterranean blood circulation systems, waterways, canalizations, rhizomatic networks—like the ancient irrigation systems spreading the water welling up from a deep source in the desert into a network that becomes oasis lushness, which is how I see Maghrebian literature as the lushness of writing in the contemporary desert of French literature—as both necessary irrigation & irritation).

And this French text is exhilarating again this morning, translating immediately (well, no, I stop & search for the English words, but I'm not "really" translating yet, I am not writing it down, it is only a part of my "reading" of Farès' text) thus immediately haltingly or haltingly immediately into some sort of English that I may or may not ever write down as a translation. I order an other coffee ("an elongated coffee," *un café allongé*, i.e. the waiter will bring the little espresso / harsh, over-roasted, certainly not the "pure Arabica" it would claim to be if I had the folly of asking after its origins / in a larger cup accompanied by a little silver pitcher of hot water with which I'll "elongate" the beverage)—an excuse, somewhere, somehow, subconsciously, to be able to lay the book down a minute, take off my glasses, eyes smart, rub them, look across the street, at the sky, still blue, but not a Mediterranean blue here in the pays d'oïl, relax the sight, but the translation machine keeps churning, I am thinking of the paragraph just read, it has the word bikini in it twice, & it should be easy to translate—but I'm not sure that it is in fact, there must be more going on here for Farès to insist on the word, putting it in caps the second time around: BIKINI. The coffee comes, I irrigate the stingy espresso with a flow of hot water, now no more need to add sugar, sip some, return to the book. Here are the sentences I've been thinking about:

Siamois II remet ses frusques. Un bikini grandeur majuscules: BIKINI. Un tricot de peau assorti aux sourcils: brousailleux.

Which, fairly straightforwardly translates as:

Siamese II puts his gear back on. A bikini of capital size: BIKINI. An undershirt matching the eyebrows: bushy, tousled.

But why, why would this weird & hilarious character (who of course has a double in the book, called Siamese I) wear a bikini. I cannot figure it out either in French or in English. What can he mean? Could it be a reference of some sort to the Bikini Islands? Nope. Just a sort of fun play on making the smallest piece of vestment women wear large, larger? A capital tiny bikini? There is nothing so far in the text that would make the "Siamese II" character a woman anyway. A transvestite? A cultural travesty of some order? All I can hear is the "bik" which could possibly go to ballpoint, in French "un bic," the writer's instrument.

Can't find it. Finish coffee, go home. Locate texts on Farès—my luck, the first one I come to cites an interview with Farès speaking about exactly these lines, this word. Farès explains to a bemused interviewer (who had also thought of the ballpoint pen!):

> Take for example what I write there in caps I AM A BIKINI There it is, written in large letters. Why do you laugh? It is one of the most important things in the book, this word BIKINI that makes you laugh!
> ... Go further: the French call us "bicots," "bics" [~ "dirty Arabs", contemp. US "towelheads", maybe closer to the n-word] I am "un bic qui nie..." / a "bic" who says no. I refuse to be a "bic"! I refuse to be subjected to the racism of the language of the French...

Untranslatable. Of course. But also, I submit, untranslatable for the French reader. Who, I am sure, will not be able to read the pun in this word any better than an English speaker. So it will be translated as bikini. A funny, startling but incomprehensible island in the language sea of Farès' narrative. The atoll I run aground on this morning. Now I can go back to my café (or maybe search out the one on rue Casimir-Delavigne that features in the chapter just before the bikini) & keep on reading. Keep on this reading that is always a translation-in-the-making, this reading-as-translation of a text that is always (okay, I'll say it: "always already") a translation.

Paris, August 2009
8/23/06

Mririda N'aït Attik
(Megdaz 1900-disappears in 1930)

THE BAD LOVER

Leave me, soldier without sense or manner !
I can see that you are full of contempt,
Your hand raised, insults on your lips,
Now that you have had what you want from me.
And you leave, calling me a dog !
Sated with my pleasures,
You'd have me blush for my trade,
But you, were you ashamed
When you pushed gently at my door,
Up like a bull ?
Were you coming to play cards ?
You turned yourself into something humble,
Agreeing right off to my demands,
To losing all your pay in advance.
And the more your eyes undressed me,
The more your rough desire put you in my power.

When you finally took off my clothes
I could have cursed your soul for the asking !
I could have cursed your mother
And your father, and their ancestors !
Toward what paradise were you flying ?

But now that you've calmed down,
You're back on earth,
Arrogant, rough & coarse as your *djellaba*.

Guest of mine for the moment, my slave,
Don't you feel my disgust & hate ?

One of these days
The Memory of tonight will bring you back to me
Conquered and submissive again.
You'll leave your pride at the door
And I'll laugh at your glances and yours wishes.
But you'll have to pay three times the price next time !
This will be the cost of your insults and pride.

I'll no more notice your clutching
Than the river notices a drop of rain.

THE BROOCH
Grandmother, grandmother,
Since he left I think only of him
And I see him everywhere.
He gave me a fine silver brooch
And when I adjust my *haïk* on my shoulders,
When I hook its flap over my breasts,
When I take it off at night to sleep,
It's not the brooch I see, but him !

My granddaughter, throw away the brooch.
You will forget him & your suffering will be over.

Grandmother, it's over a month since I threw it away,
But it cut deeply into my hand.
I can't take my eyes off the red scar :
When I wash, when I spin, when I drink
And my thoughts are still of him !

My granddaughter, may Allah heal your pain !
The scar is not on your hand, but in your heart.

COMMENTARY

Mririda n'Ait Attik was a Moroccan poet composing in Tashelhiyt Berber. She was born around 1900 in Megdaz in the Tassaout valley. Her poems were put to paper & translated into French in the 1930s by René Euloge, a French civil servant based in Azila from 1927, in his book *Les chants de la Tassout*. Our selection is based on an English version of Euloge's work, *Songs of Mririda Courtesan of the High Atlas*, translated by Daniel Halpern & Paula Paley from the French version (Unicorn Press, 1974).

Abdellatif Laâbi : So many betweens!

> I'm not the nomad
> searches for the well
> the sedentary has dug,
> I drink little water
> and walk
> apart from the caravan.
>
> Abdellatif Laâbi

In 1966 the great German-language poet Paul Celan, an exile living in Paris, France, called his new book of poems, to come out the following year, *Atemwende*, compounding the nouns for breath & change; that same year, a young Moroccan poet by the name of Abdellatif Laâbi (born in the city of Fez in 1942) called his newly founded magazine, *Souffles*, meaning "Breath" in the plural. I translated Celan's title as *Breathturn*, i.e. a turning of, a change of, the breath. Something—poem, movement, event—that wants to bring real change, does, has to, take the breath away in order to effect this change & in the same movement, it—poem or event—gives new directions to one's (next) breath—one's pneuma, the systole/diastole that is the one certain way we know that we are alive. In Morocco, Laâbi & friends wanted & needed to draw many free, new & unsettling breaths, *des souffles*—& the magazine by that name indeed did just that & was immediately & has remained until today the great North African avant-garde poetry magazine of the period. In Paris, Mohamed Khair-Eddine showed me a copy just before I embarked for America in late 1967 & I realized immediately that if poetry in French was to be again of essential use it would need to be retooled there, in a Maghreb struggling to create itself as a new, independent & revolutionary society, far away from Paris living on its pre-war modernisms. *Souffles* took one's breath away, heralding the changes being made in Maghrebian poetry while proposing changes that needed to be made in the life of the people—that is, it could not but be a politically revolutionary magazine too. The absolute seriousness of Laâbi & his friends concerning this need for change, for an *Atemwende* at every level did not escape the notice of the powers that be, & the magazine was eventually censored & in 1972 Laâbi was jailed, tortured & submitted to all the humiliations a dictatorship will submit its opponents to. Abdellatif survived, kept writing poems, letters, prose, essays, producing a continuous & courageous witnessing to his & this society's fate. In 1980 he was released & in 1985 he moved to Paris, France where he still lives most of the time, in that permanent exile that seems to be the lot of so many of the century's best poets & doers—a poet, from Greek "poesis" to make, to do, is or should be, & in Laâbi's case is, indeed, a doer, an activist. In recent years he has been able to return & live part of the time in Morocco, though this is not without its dangers, as some painful misadventures two years ago prove.

*

Abdellatif Laâbi is without a doubt the major francophone voice in Moroccan poetry today. It may—& does, especially for some of the arabophone poets of the Maghreb & the Mashreq—bring up the question of why should a Moroccan author write in the colonial language after his country's independence? The most forceful way I have heard this question answered is by the Algerian poet & novelist Kateb Yacine who, when asked by journalists after Algeria gained its independence in 1962 following an 8 year war, if he would now write in Arabic, responded: "We won the war. We'll keep French as the spoils of war." Kateb went on to say that for a Maghrebian to write in Arabic would simply be to submit to an earlier, if more acculturated colonial domination, given that the autochthonous cultures are Berber with their own languages (Tamazight) & writing (Tifinak). Be that as it may, the multilingualism of the Maghreb has made for a very rich, multi-layered tapestry of writing and, as I have shown elsewhere, it is exactly in those ex-colonies or ex-protectorates that an enriched French has made for a poetry more impressive than the relatively pale "metropolitan" version. Abdellatif Laâbi's language is proof of this.

He writes with a quiet, unassuming elegance that holds & hides the violence any act of creation proposes. Every creation is of course a breaking apart, a making of fragments—making *is* breaking—something Laâbi states *ab initio* in his poem "Forgotten Creation": "In the beginning was the cry / & already discord." And this poem—as does most of his vast oeuvre—follows the movements of this cry, tracing its starts & stops, circling its essential enigma, descrying all the false mysteries & hopes & fantasies it gives rise to, despite itself. Creating itself, the poem learns that "where nothing is born / nothing changes," & that eternity is but "an impenetrable jar / no magic will open." But the poem, Laâbi insists, will get us inside this act of imaginative creation. It is exactly the processual nature of his poetics, demanding a close listening to both inside & outside worlds, & the will & courage to follow changing meanders as the outside historical situation & the personal ecology of the poet's world evolve, at times clash, but always inform—taking careful account of both the "in" & the "form" the word proposes—his work.

If the one constant in Laâbi's life has been writing—in the early prison volume *Between the Gag, the Poem* he framed it thus: "Write, write, never stop"—it is however also clear that there has been an evolution throughout his writing career. The earlier work shows all the outward projective force & explosive power the discovery of revolutionary possibilities immediately succeeded by the experience of injustice, jail & torture under a profoundly flawed & paranoid political system entails. The drive, jaggedness, mutilated syntax, dissociative, near-surreal & explosive verse associating a sharply analyzed exterior world & a internal turmoil & questioning is not without reminding the reader of some of the writings of the American Beat poets: this is indeed a Maghrebi "Howl." It is interesting to note, as Laâbi did on the occasion of a meeting earlier this year, that at that time he & the *Souffles* writers were unaware of the American poetry scene, & thus of the Beats & other "protest poetry" which they were to discover only some time later. They were however knowledgeable about avant-garde traditions in European & especially French poetry from Rimbaud on through the surrealists, and, given their political readings, of some of the Russian avant-garde & of poets such as Pablo Neruda & Nazim Hikmet.

If over the years Laâbi has also produced a range of prose works—from novels, memoirs, tales & essays to plays & several volumes of interviews—poetry has clearly been the guiding light of his work. It is in following the changes the decades brought about in his poetics, that we can trace Laâbi's development, which has morphed from the early work described above to a quieter, lyrical voice—quieter, but in no way less searching, less demanding, less questing. The volumes of the last ten years may look deceptively simple at the level of their lyric line & language at quick glance (though the multi- or at least double-cultured metaphors remain often stunningly potent), but don't pre-judge: this is in no way a self-satisfied *Altenstil*; this is, rather, the calm, easy-breathing simplicity of achieved yet always again questioned wisdom, after a life of struggle. Maybe one should think about Laâbi's achievement here as Blakean, at the level of both poesis & lived life: it is the clarity of an innocence regained, with much exertion, after having gone through all the experience a human can take. It is the achieving of alchemical gold after many decades of labor in the double pelican of life & writing.

My own attraction to Laâbi's work over the years has been rooted in my fascination for what I've come to call "betweeness," that state of exile (voluntary or not), of one's de facto multi-lingual (& thus non-linear) space in a post-colonial situation (& I'd argue that we all are post-colonials to some extent). Here is how he defined this space of betweenness some twenty years ago:

> I truly feel myself located on this hinge of being between life & death..., between a sun that is dying & another one whose rising has been confiscated, between two planets, two humanities that turn their backs to each other, between the feminine part in myself & my status as a male (which however has no desire to change gender), between two cultures that don't stop misapprehending each other, two languages that speak themselves so continuously in my mouth that they make me stammer, between the madness of hope & despair's just returns, between a country of origin that dribbles away & another country, an adopted one, that isn't able to firm itself, between a "natural" tendency toward meditation & an irrepressible need for action, between belonging & non-belonging, nomadism & sedentariness... So many betweens!

And Laâbi, in his life & in his work, has shown us the elegance & graciousness it takes to accomplish this task. What it takes to reside in this betweenness is negative capability, i.e. (in Shelley's word) "when a man is capable of being in uncertainties, mysteries, doubts, without any irritable reaching after fact & reason." For Laâbi that means, for example, to see the question of "identity" as something that is "more of a project than something acquired at birth." Culturally & ideologically this is of great importance in his world—where the culture given at birth is a knot of religion & politics that cannot be untangled—& in which "identitarism is one of the oldest & most insidious forms of integrism," which makes "voluntary servitude the price of belonging."

What makes this path in-between so many in-betweens walkable, livable? How does this manifold doubleness not end up simply becoming a permissive fog in which one gets lost, voluntarily or involuntarily—or act outside the view of the world? Laâbi has been clear that his essential battle has been the one he fights against the hiatus between discourse & praxis, between thought & action, between the work—including that of *poesis,* of poetry—& the man. As he puts it: "For me ethics is the basis of politics as much as of literature or thinking." It is this struggle, what he calls his "solitary-solidary struggle," deeply committed, deeply political, yet situated outside any ideological system, a struggle toward the construction of an ethics able to equal the complexities of our world, that has been his compass.

The rest is poetry.

Pierre Joris, Brooklyn-Paris /May/June 2016
Forward for *In Praise of Defeat* (archipelago press 2017)

THE SONG OF THE AZRIA

I am beautiful Azria
I am unfaithful Azria
I am the tender fruit
of a tree with tight clusters
I smile at everyone
I hate marriage
& for no prize
will I admit slavery
I wear no veil
I hate all cloth
my happiness is
beauty & youth
my black eyes'
mysterious gaze
has the power
to enthrall my lovers
my Queen Kahina face
is more than bait
my mouth is made of honey
perfectly real
he who tastes it once
will return for more
my chest & its high breasts
draws in the holiest looks
while below my belt
lies nature's sacred temple
where the faithful come to sin
in love my heart
often lies for
I am Azria
remorseless Azria

I accept the weak & the strong
I am carefree Azria
& my life is my life
my pride comes from my freedom
my life is crazy gaiety
from the most noble to the ugliest
my lovers are innumerable
I am Azria the dancer
who makes women jealous
I am the singer
I am the crooner
my gorgeous voice
opens all doors

   Adapted by P.J. from Y Georges Kerhuel's version

COMMENTARY

This eponymous song, arranged by Y. Georges Kerhuel & included in the *Encyclopédie de l'amour en islam Tome 1* (edit. Malek Chabel), speaks to the specific situation of Shawia Berber society of the Aurès mountains (Northeastern Algeria). Mathéa Gaudry, a lawyer at the Appellate Court in Algiers, wrote about the Shawia courtesans in a treatise on Aurès culture in the 1920s: "The power of the Shawia woman does not pale with time. Knowledge of occult sciences, the prerogative of the elder, only reinforces it. [...] The azria is a courtesan who received who she wants & goes where she wants. She sings, dances, plays cards, smokes & goes to cafés. No triviality in her manners; to the contrary: a tranquil self-assurance & often a natural distinction are her mark. Her courtiers' enthusiasm surrounds her. They all show her a quasi-religious submission. When she intervenes, a fight will stop immediately."

FEZ—
City through Time & Space

A city is time. All the time. All the times. Slow, fast. Viscous, smooth. Chronopolis.

These are but first notes towards a longer something on Fez, the Moroccan city & its articulations through its history, architecture & literature over time. I spent a fair amount of time in this city over the years & want to, need to return, or better, to turn around this city set in a bowl in the shadow of Zalagh mountain, again & again, as it is one of the places in the world—at least as far as I know—that most fascinatingly combines the oldest & the newest. How to write today about a place like Fez raises the question of genre: what kind of essay, if it is an essay, is this to be? An ethnographic essay? A theoretico-critical construct? Or a chronicle? A traveler's diary or "relacion" or, maybe more accurately, a "riḥla" as the Arabic travelogue is called? But I could not open my rihla the way Ibn Battuta did his:

> I left Tangiers, my birthplace on Thursday, 2nd Rahab, 725 [14 June 1325] being at that time twenty two years of age, with the intention of making the Pilgrimage to the Holy House [at Mecca] & the tomb of the Prophet [at Madina]. I set out alone, finding no companion to cheer the way with friendly intercourse, & no party of travelers with whom to associate.

No religious pilgrimage is implied in my travelogues, even if there was indeed a moment of true awe on my last visit, when a Fassi friend showed me a small, tilting, heavily braced structure & told me that this was where Ibn Arabi, *el sheikh el-akhbar*, had worshipped & spent daily time in, during the two years he lived in Fez. It was here that Ibn Arabi finished a major text, *Al Kitab al-isrá, The Book of the Night Journey* in 1198. This was another travelogue, but, as Claude Addas writes in his *Ibn Arabi et le voyage sans retour* (Le Seuil, 1996), one "whose title—the word *isrá*, night journey—locates it squarely in the Islamic tradition where the term alludes to the episode in Mohammed's life when the latter was miraculously transported one night from Mecca to Jerusalem & from Jerusalem to the Divine Throne, thus to a distance of 'two bow shots or less' (Quran, 52:9) from the deity. Ibn Arabi maintains in *Al Kitab al-isrá* that this trip is not reserved for the Prophet—that his 'inheritors' can do it as well, with this difference: while Mohammed did the trip physically, the inheritors can only do it mentally/spiritually." Claude Addas again: "A vertical journey thus, but a *nocturnal* one: it is only when he has disappeared in the night of his ontological indigence that the contemplative encounters the One without a second."

Be that as it may, during my stays in Fez I mainly wrote poems, plus a few pages of diaristic notes on the town & the people I met, as well as a number of letters to my close ones back "home" & many emails to various friends & acquaintances, and, finally took some 200 photographs which remain uncatalogued to this day. How to consolidate all those already written & visualized takes plus what the process of reading & thinking about Fez brings up? For the occasion, & not wanting to start with a tourist map, let me try a little act of the imagination.

First, THE OUTSIDE. If Salvador Dali had designed an hourglass—though in this case its other name, based on what runs through it, may be more apposite, i.e. the sandglass or sand timer—he could have done worse than to inspire himself with the shape of Fez: Fez-el-Bali, the old medina, the oldest medieval town still in full socio-political function (the historical & spiritual capital, even if Rabat is the modern bureaucratic capital), is the top bulb or upper reservoir. The lower reservoir would be the *Ville Nouvelle*, the New Town built on the baking plain to the south-west of Fez-el-Bali by the French starting in the early years of the protectorate, & still expanding today. In between, the "goulot d'étranglement," literally the stranglehold bottle-neck, is Fez el Djedid, or New Fez, which at its narrowest point, where it links to New Town, consists of one large 4-lane car-artery in the center, a smaller vein running east of it & the train tracks running west of center through meadows beloved by the 100s of storks that live in Fez.

Strategically situated at the narrowest point, on a small plateau, an open space visible from both bulbs, there is a large rectangular parking lot with at its center a square restaurant straddling the times: shaded, outside tables, belonging to an older Mediterranean (if not necessarily an architecturally fassi) dispensation arrayed on all sides of a square building recognizable everywhere even if the tall neon Arab script on the golden arches didn't announce it as a McDonald's. Though there is no " ' " in the Arabic word as spelled out on the sign, the final possessive "s" of its English grammatical mode has been faithfully, incongruously & meaninglessly transcribed into the Arab letter "sin" directly attached to the "daad." In the translation of the name, the possessive quality has been made invisible, lies hidden in the transcription as a meaningless "ess" sound—the hissing snake of late capitalism?—bringing to mind Frantz Fanon's observation that "the business of obscuring language is a mask behind which stands out the much greater business of plunder."

But how much is this critique of US commercial ventures based on personal vexation? Isn't it true that one reason to travel outside this country is to finally find a place where all is not the same, architecturally & commercially speaking? (Remembering here too my immense annoyance when in Beijing I finally reached the heart of the old Forbidden City, the hidden secret center of the Kingdom of the Middle, only to discover right smack in that bull's eye a well-known Seattle based coffee-shop franchise.) And for sure, the Fassis may not like the American-ness of the McDonald's, but they like the modernity of it—especially those from the lower bulb, the French built New Town; the inhabitants of the upper bulb, Fez-el-Bali, economically poorer in the majority, & as conscious inhabitants of an old medina, will frown more at their children's demand to be taken there—though many will give in & bus it or walk over on a holiday for a McDo—as people are want to say here, using the French language filter & hip abbreviation the old colonial metropole—as invaded as Morocco by US franchises—uses.

And so, from the skewed perspective of the balcony of my hotel room in the New Town I see the neon sign of the Macdonald's right there hanging like a cut-throat menace over the bottleneck of my Daliesque Fez-as-sandglass—or maybe it can be read as a sort of Maxwell's demon, sorting out the traffic from the old to the new, from the new to the old, creating & upholding a line of separation that cuts the city at least in two, with the small red taxis, the cheapest means of moving around the town, as visual red corpuscles pulsing through the city's arteries.

But then this city—like many other cities—has always thrived, has in fact be born out of, such a doublet as new & old town. As soon as you draw a line you may create a universe, as Spencer Brown suggests in his book *Laws of Form*, as you inscribe a difference, you will have created a left side & a right side, rive gauche, rive droite as they say in Paris, East side, West side as they say in New York. You may not even have to draw the line, it may be given you by the topography of the place. Here in Fez it is the river & so, from the very beginning on the city was always double: the mythologo-historical first Kings, Idris 1 & Idris 2, are said to have both founded the city—what is now Fez-el-Bali—each on opposite banks of the river in the 9C century, so that there always already were two Fez's to begin with—(& thus Fez=axe, splitting instrument, maybe the two-bladed Cretan axe?) something that perpetuated itself through time, as the first wave of immigrants came from the East, maybe from as far away as Arabia, & settled on the eastern shore of the river, while the next wave of immigrants coming from the north, from Al Andalus, settled on the western side of the river. In bad years the fighting between the people inhabiting the two sides of the river could be so fierce that the river was no longer enough as a border-separation & so the inhabitants built a wall right down the middle of the city. This was so during the Almoravid & Almohad periods, i.e. until the middle of the 13C. When the Merenids — Berbers from the Beni Merin tribe—captured Fez, the Fassis never took to this new dynasty who to them were mere Berber chiefs of a nomad tribe from the eastern plains. So much so that Abu Yusuf Yaqub who reigned from 1259 to 1286, didn't feel secure enough to dwell among the citizens in the city on the two river banks, & in 1276 started work on Fez Jedid, the New Fez, enclosing this new city—a compound of palatial & administrative buildings—in a double wall 750 meters away from Fez-el-Bali. A bit later on he had the interior wall of the old Medina, built previously along the river, torn down—to make Fez-al-Bali one again & to simultaneously insist on the new doubleness Old/New-Fez.

All of this constant growth by mirroring, doubling, in- & ex-folding needs to be further thought through—& can be visualized through the three distinctive architectural styles that define the current triple layout of the city: old traditional housing (narrow alleyways, blind alleys galore, blind house walls with only one opening for a door, that gives on the inner court letting sun & light in, etc.) in Fez-el-Bali; later classic Arab architecture of the palatial & military kind with Ottoman & Occidental influences in Fez Djedid; & colonial French & modern architecture in the *Ville Nouvelle*. All three of these stages are, however, totally alive & functioning now in the present—& the three styles have of course also given rise to a range of hybrid structures that would be worth analyzing in some detail. (UNESCO has declared Fez-el-Bali a "historical" town & is helping to restore it—which of course involves sordid tales involving money, power-brokers & all the King's men: too long & complicated a story to tell here now.)

The history of Fez is the unfolding, the dedoubling of these urban spaces under mainly outside impulses (the inside, those who live inside the walls, tend to want to keep things on an even keel, unchanging, if possible, though it never is possible.) At this point in the final full *son-et-lumière* presentation you would here a voice in Arabic reading extracts from the *Nashr al-mathani, The Chronicles* of Muhammad al-Qadiri, the historian of Fez born in that city in 1712 & dying there in 1773, while an English version of the text would scroll by on the screen, alternating with English voice/Arabic text. Here are a few excerpts from this text, in an English translation by Norman Cigar, to give a flavor of Fassi historiography:

> 1085/1674-1675
>
> Among the events of this year was the burning down in Fez of seventeen shops in Suq al-'Attarin al-Kubra, with the consequent collapse of its walls & great loss of property. I do not know what caused it, but a short time later there was a similar fire in the very same place, when even more shops were burned down. This one was caused by one of the mirror-makers who left a lit brazier in his shop, in which there was sulphur, & this was ignited by the flame during the night.

Now, what is truly interesting here is that, in the margins of al-Qadiri's ms., a later (but not too late) copyist has added a further note, clarifying the incident: "There was gun-powder in one of the shops, & its owner was smoking, A spark from the tobacco flew from the pipe which was in the mouth, onto the powder, causing a great explosion in the shop, God knows best." History is indeed a palimpsest of writings, a visual construct too. Al-Qadiri goes on:

> 1085/1674-1675
> On Saturday morning, 14 Rajab (14 Oct. 1674), the sons of Yafrah were executed & their corpses paraded through the streets of Fez, since they had done their best to induce the city of Fez to revolt against Moulay Ismail. Once Fez had fallen, they had fled to a certain mountain, but he got the better of them & put them to death. They were from the people of Figuig who had originally gone to Andalusia & had emigrated after the 'Misfortune', settling in Qarawiyyin Fez.

Meaning on the right bank, the bank of the Andalusian emigrants—& thus the historiographer keeps the old separations & family kinship lines alive across the centuries. If history—& I could have given many more examples from Al-Qadiri's Chronicles (there's a wonderful single sentence chronicle for what must have been a happy year, the year 1695 that reads in its entirety: "Among this year's events was a violent windstorm which, however, caused no damage.")—if history is the tale of what happens to the city with most of that coming from the outside, let's look however also if ever so briefly to the inside of the city.

If we try to read Fez closer to us, it may come as a surprise that maybe the best "text" dealing with modern Fez is a novel written by a foreigner—the American Paul Bowles—even if the book in question, *The Spider's House* is rarely considered one of the author's major books. And yet, I think it a major achievement, even if against Bowles' own preferences. He had wanted to write an apolitical book, in fact a book without any sense of a "chronopolitics"—i.e. a generic tale of his usual foreign wanderers in some heart of darkness, in this case picturesque Fez—but as he was writing the book, history took over. Here is how he spoke of this in the 1981 introduction to the 1955 book:

> I wanted to write a novel using as backdrop the traditional daily life of Fez, because it was a medieval city functioning in the twentieth century. If I had started it only one year sooner it would have been an entirely different book. I intended to describe Fez as it existed at the moment of writing about it, but even as I started to write, events that could not be ignored had begun to occur there. I soon saw that I was going to have to write, not about the traditional pattern of life in Fez, but about its dissolution.

Which is of course not really true: the "traditional life of Fez" has for a millennium been riddled with political & cultural upheavals & the events that will mark the beginning of the end of the French colonial days are in that sense not absolutely different from other moments of political turmoil. But Bowles has otherwise excellent insight into what was happening, even if he came to it against his desire. He had thus hoped for the end of French rule in Morocco with as much intensity as the Moroccans, though he, the American, had hoped & believed that after Independence "the old manner of life would be resumed & the country would return to be more or less what it had been before the French presence." What he had failed to understand, as he writes in the preface, "was that if Morocco was still largely a medieval land, it was because the French themselves, & not the Moroccans wanted it that way." But this modernization has not necessarily destroyed the "medieval" parts of the city, it may in fact be that it is paradoxically only through modernisation that the medieval city can survive—while the lower bulb of my sand clock, the *Ville Nouvelle,* is now reaching exorbitant proportions.

Here, a few short extracts in which Stenham, the American visitor in Bowles' book, is walked back to his hotel at night through the medina by a Berber guide:

> Now & then he had the distinct impression that they were traversing a street or an open space that he knew perfectly well, but if that were so, the angle at which they had met it was unexpected, so that the familiar walls (if indeed they *were* familiar walls) were dwarfed or distorted in the one swiftly fading beam of light he played on them.

As counterbalance to Bowles' Fez, I would suggest the Fez of Abdellatif Laâbi's youth, as remembered by the poet in his 2002 book *Le Fond de la Jarre*[7]—a totally delightful childhood memoir, & in Laâbi's work the opposite of his life in Rabat & the Meknes prison.

To conclude this all too brief introduction, no, panegyric, to Fez let me read you this extract from the Tunisian writer Abdelwahab Meddeb's book *Aya dans les Villes*. It is a single sentence, a fast walk covering maybe three hundred yards down the main thoroughfare south starting from the Karouyin mosque. It is part of a sequence that travels in such single-sentence-writing with a sweeping movement through Fez, covering, I would suggest the same distance & in a related manner, that Orson Wells' camera covers in that amazing opening shot of *A Touch of Evil*—& has the same paradoxical form: one single movement that crosses over from Mexico into the US, just as Meddeb's writing in a single run-on stroke crosses from Old Fez to New Fez.

So here, a pen as fast as any camera:

---

[7] Now available in English as *The Bottom of the Jar* (translated by André Naffis-Sahely, archipelago books, 2013.

The gaze in movement fixes on a mosque which exchanges the pillars and arcs of masonry bricks, coated and whitewashed, for wooden cornices and pilasters, beams and posts that introduce an Anatolian orthogonality unknown in a city so close to the Atlas mountains whose animated street stalls propose the evening soup and attendant sweets, in the continuation of the huge blind walls only occasionally pierced by very small loopholes, beyond the corner the wall swelling out into a human sized apsis that juts forward, reverse of a mirhab cluttering the passage, to the small oratory links to the dark shed with the stretch of a barrel vaulting, long and narrow, a depository transformed into a movie theater programming Egyptian and Hindu films, a quavering bell announces the imminent start of the next performance, the eye scours the multiple yellow spots of the lamps dotting the approaching darkness in a line that leads to the noisy café of the keefed ones, the front of the place garnished with large tin cans, flower pots and odiferous plants, next to multiple cages made of jonquils housing birds tamed for their song, the doves coo, the canaries interlace their arpeggios, while the nose succumbs to the scents of basil and carnations, which chase mosquitoes and invite the angels incarnated as ephebes satisfying the eye of the onlookers who tango on waves of nostalgia.

Cheikha Rimitti
(Oran region, 1920- Paris, 2006)

THE GIRLS OF BEL-ABBES

my love, I've heard your call, how far away it seemed to be.

we are the girls of Bel-Abbès, we are not lost girls
I'll make a pilgrimage to Sidi el Hadri & he'll give me a child
my reason has left me, carried away by the son of Maïcha

death? we'll all die, only god will remain
the black horse's forelock brings luck
engraved on my love's pistol, a star & a crescent

in the green door's frame Zohra arches her back
her blonde hair falls over her white flesh
lala la la la....

THE WORST OF ALL SHELTERS

exile, my friend, goes hand in hand with hard patience
ah! the worst of all shelters!
my hair's turned white
the days have gone under & are forgotten
now I want a roof of my own
but the douar is deserted, only ruins remain
this beautiful assembly's dispersed
oh! the return to the old place!
my hair's turned white
my friends, had you suffered like me, you'd understand
many men are missing
only buildings remain

oh! the return to the old place!
white farm, green olive trees
those brave olive trees, oh my men!
the oil of the olive, the fish in the sea
there's bravery, oh my men!
I remember those who're absent
oh! the return to the old place!
may God take into his peace those who've died for the country
oh! The return to the old place! Oh! My land!
falling, he yelled: mother's family house is in ruins!
let's intercede for the parents & the heroes
the parents, the parents
my father & my mother cursed me. oh it's hard it's hard!
do not forget the parents
take care of your parents, & they'll bless you
me, I weep on exile, o you men!
I weep on exile, homesickness squeezes the heart in France
oh my men! oh my friends!
may god give patience to those who are in France
oh my men! oh my friends!
exile's called & dispersed the assemblies
ah! the worst of all shelters!
the worst of all shelters!
oh my friends!

COMMENTARY

Cheikha Rimitti was the grand old lady of ur-raï music & one of the great voices of the 20th century. Writes Marie Virolle in *La chanson raï*: "Vernacular Algerian Arabic cries in Rimitti's throat, popular culture weeps in Rimitti's songs, the poetry Western Algeria vibrates in Rimitti's voice.... Family feasts, brotherhood events, studios, galas, salons, forests, hangars, cabarets, cafés, tents, terraces, on warm earth under starry skies, no place where one sings with the people was foreign to her." Rimitti—who got her name from the French word "remettez-moi ça" meaning "pour me another round"—& started singing in bars & other places of ill repute, had learned singing at the rigorous school of the beduin melhun qacida. Her first major success was also her first (but not last) major thematic innovative breakthrough, a scandalous manifesto-song called "Charrak gattaa" / "Tear it, Rip it!" & which goes on: "... & Rimitti will sew it up again / Let's do our things beneath the covers / move after move / I'll do whatever my lover wants / I fell for the wholesaler in fruit / the one with the dove on the turban /..." easy enough to hear the title as referring to virginity & the song as a rebellious call for free love in a puritan islamic society. At her last concert 2 days before she died—she was in her early 80s—at the *Zénith* in Paris, she was carried off stage in triumph—or she may have sung all night long.

Translated from a French version by P.J.

On the Nomadic Circulation of Contemporary Poetics between Europe, North America & the Maghreb

In the poem "Ode or Nearly There" from *h.j.r.* a line wrote itself: "[To] caravan / atoms into lines of flight." The oddness of that line was brought home—wherever that may be, if ever caravans do get there, which is, in turn, neither here nor there—when it was queried by my French translator. Though French certainly isn't home either, as no language is, despite our desire to make it so. Language is the stranger, the other, we want to engage & which always, & irremediably so, remains the outside. Our outside we are building a future home in which we will never inhabit. We can only inhabit that which will disappear with us, that which does not survive us, i.e. ourselves. We are our home, the infinitesimal second—*die Sekunde, diese Kunde*—of presence to ourselves we imagine in retrospect to have been us present to ourselves when we / it is already too late, gone, a cadaver as we move into a here that, even before we can dot the I of our quasi-presence, has become a there. A there that does not "exist," that is always already an ex- if it "ist" at all, but really, neither back there nor ahead, as René Daumal says: "J'avance vers un avenir qui n'existe pas. I am going towards a future that does not exist: leaving every minute a new corpse behind me." His was a slower time, this giddy fin-de-siècle makes that every second. "Sirrt die Sekunde." Atom of time. One by one, second to none. Uncuttable: from Latin *secare*, to cut, or split. The deepest cut. And uncuttable sequence. Daumal's minute may be tropologically meant to stand for the minutest, but it is still a molar comfort.

These are the languages of my dispersals, my diasporic wanderings, the German & the French that underlie the lingua franca of the new empire: American English. The omitted first, or degree zero language, really, of my languages: *Letzebuergesch*, a gentle ghosting appearing at times in certain s-sounds, in the impossible "tee-aitch" where "so" & "though" become homophonic, & the sh-sounds, sschlupping about, but hush now, that's the mamalaschen, so far removed now though so far from removed that I sometimes fear it will come back in the last words it will be given me to speak & that no one will then be able to understand. And finally there is the Arabic that has gone missing, that I chase after, promising myself to make it yet into the tent where late in the day when the sun is setting over the schist mountains of Thamad sung by Ibn Tarafa, all the others can gather to enjoy the hospitality of that nomadicity I have made so much of. (We may then again discuss what Derrida thought so often about, identity, ipseity, & the "pse" of "ipse" more than the initial "I" & its dissemination through that range of terms that create an Indo-European complex which puts hospitality & hostility under the same tent. And then we will wonder if under the tent of Arabic hospitality—*ziyafah*—where I hear, ignorant of the etymology right now, certain phrases, i.e. you have to show it, hospitality, ziyafah, to everyone, to the stranger as well, to the one on the road, & will of course link up with Derrida's wanderings around the hostis/hospes theme. It is exactly when Derrida begins to think his diasporic self, his Franco-Maghrebian non-identity, his worried, threatened, recent, precarious citizenship, that he proposes the *monolingualism of the Other* with its double, contradictory postulation:

—*We only ever speak one language...*
(yes but)
—*We never speak only one language...*

And this, interestingly enough, immediately gets Derrida to think of that most diasporic act of crossing, translation, as he writes that this double postulation "is not only the very law of what is called translation. It would also be the law itself as translation." A core diasporic performance for writers is of course translation—first in their own writing, in the written "monolingualism" of their books, & then in the translations—& their attending problems—these books, are rather the "language(s)" of these books posit.

What I want to do in the following is to posit a few markers to witness this contemporary complexity. The growing nomadicity of our languages, the dissemination of minor-literature modes as Deleuze-Guattari like to call them, the critical reflection elaborated by theorists/writers such as the Algerian Reda Bensmaïa, or the Martinican poet/theorist Edouard Glissant (cf. his *Introduction à une poétique du divers*, & his *Poetics of Relation*) & the cultural practices of post-colonial poets, thinkers & translators all contribute to a radical subversion of traditional cultural patterns in both writing & translating. Here then a quick sketch of a few of the vectors these new diasporic practices take through the work of four Maghrebian writers—Abdelwahab Meddeb (Tunisia), Habib Tengour (Algeria), Driss Chraïbi & Abdelkebir Khatibi (Morocco). This will be a heterogeneous meander, as I will use their work to bring up a variety of questions, problems, matters, really that will however not coalesce into some wider picture. Archipelago-poetics, archipelago-politics.

Driss Chraïbi, the elder statesmen of the modern Moroccan—Maghrebian, really—novel, startled & upset his country (while gaining immediate recognition in France) when in 1954, just two years before Moroccan independence, he published his first novel *Le Passé Simple* in Paris, France. This is a paradigmatic work stating the epistemic break between traditional (Arabo-Islamic) Moroccan culture & the modernity of French-speaking culture in terms of the family genealogy of a father/son opposition. Let me just touch upon two aspects that highlight tiny, but essential matters regarding the situation of the Maghrebian (writer) & his *langue fourchue*, his "forked tongue," to use Abdelfattah Kilito's expression, in relation to writing & translation: first, the title & then the problem of a possible/impossible return to the language of the country after independence. *Le Passé Simple* is not only *in* French but speaks *of* & *to* French—in that its surface semantic meaning is (literally translated) "The Simple Past" (the English translation of the book is called just that), while for any French-speaker educated in his or her language, the phrase is immediately & simultaneously heard as the grammatical name it also is: the past historic tense. Writes Stefania Pandolfo in her essay "The Thin Line of Modernity":

> The French passé simple, grammatically, is the tense of an impossible narration. Rarely used in the first person & almost untranslatable in English (*je fûs*, "I have been," but in the remote past, a past forever severed from myself), the passé simple conveys without mediation the uncanny temporality of a cut. ("The thin line..."p 119)

Obviously Chraïbi wanted to inscribe this "uncanny temporality of a cut" into his title. This is exactly the paradoxical nature of these three words: the semantic surface simplicity of the simple noun qualified (*le passé*) by a descriptive adjective (*simple*) is undercut, torn apart by the *other* meaning, the one that states exactly the opposite, namely that this past is in fact not simple at all, but inscribes a cut, a fracture, the wound that will not heal, the aporia of an active absence/presence in the "simple" title. It may be going too far to see in this title the (unintended?) ghosting of Arabic (something we will come back to in more detail when speaking of Abdelwahab Meddeb's work). Or at least of one aspect of Arabic poetics, namely the traditional use in popular poems of words whose polysemic meanings include the exact opposite of the stated, surface meaning. Such a device was very useful indeed in an autocratic society where the poet could (and had to) address laudatory epithets to the sovereign, as it enabled the poet to reveal in the same word the hidden truth of despotic oppression. Be that as it may, it does seem important to me to insist on the fact that the poetics of Chraïbi's French title rehearse, while displacing, the initial & initiating Maghrebi wound of the forked tongue: here, rather than playing itself out between Arabic & French, the cut is (re)located in the other's language itself. The colonizer's language too is caught in an irresolvable double bind: no language is a house the writer can simply inhabit, the only home is to found in the ever-shifting force field of the spaces of its internal contradictions—which it is the writer's job to bring to light.

Obviously the English title "The Simple Past" completely strips away that cut, that trauma expressly stated, demanded by the French title, leaving a nearly quietist, pastoral sense of "simplicity." (cf. Flaubert's title : *Un coeur simple*/ *A Simple Heart*) What would happen if the title were translated into Arabic? I nearly wrote "back into Arabic"—but a back is unwarranted, Chraïbi wrote from & into French, that is the whole point of the book— the novel's own desire is to be an accurate temporal arrow, forward from the old Arabo-Islamic tradition to the modernity of the colonizing civilization. Now, despite the furor the book caused when it was published, it did eventually return to the (Arabic) Maghreb, even if by a circuitous route: it is only one of two Chraïbi novels translated into Arabic, but published in Tunisia, not Morocco—thus returning from the diasporic language but not (yet) to the homeland. But there is a further twist: the Arabic title of *Le Passé Simple* becomes, just as the English, literally *The Simple Past* i.e. it makes for the same reduction than the englished title —an irony one could read as yet another proof of the impossibility of translation. At one level then, Chraïbi "cannot go home again," at another, this impossibility can be read as the basic law of nomadicity & of a diasporic poetics: the eternal return to an original site can only locate change, abolish itself, find the new as the ruins of the old, as the ruined origin. It is as if the most modern situation of the Maghrebian writer mirrored the opening of the oldest poems: the *atlal* or return to last year's camp-fire, there only as ruins, as trace. We will return & stop there too.

The second point I want to make concerning Driss Chraïbi's work, & of further interest in this context, is the fact that a later novel by Chraïbi, *Un ami viendra vous voir?* (1966) also caused scandal, but this time on both sides of the Mediterranean & for the same reason: refusing or trying to overcome the wound of the forked tongue at least at the level of content, the novel did not speak of either Maghreb or France, but was set in Canada & thus eschewed any of the thematics expected from a "Franco-Maghrebian" work. Double scandal! Writes Abdellatif Abboubi:

> By writing *Un Ami viendra vous voir*, Chraïbi aimed at destroying, proof in hand, some of the base prejudices shared by a society undermined by racism & the exclusion of the other; & notably those clichés anchored in the imaginary of a Parisian elite stuck in the swamp of its superiority complex, & which considers literature & art according to ideas based on geograhical belonging (*sol*) & race. An idea which gains a white writer, newly arrived from Argentina or Russia, for example, easy admission into the small club of Parisian literati. By contrast, the writers coming from the ex-colonies found themselves parked in a narrow square full of obstacles & traps. Simply because they were of arabo-african origin. (my translation)

In a fascinating return, it is this novel that has just this past year been published in an Arabic translation by Abdellatif Abboudi in Morocco.

I have so far spoken of novels (or at least of the title of a novel), rather than of poetry, & this stands to reason: the genre with which the Maghrebi writers first advanced their cause in French & in France was the novel—a Western form that was unknown in the Arab context—& not poetry, the essential literary form of the Arab-speaking peoples. Though a study of the other founding maghrebin novel, Kateb Yacine's *Nedjma*, would show that in his writing the notion of genre is itself completely nomadic: the "novel" *Nedjma* can—& should, in fact —be seen as but one moment (what I have elsewhere called a "mawqif," a station, a momentary stopping point) of a vast katebian "écriture" that constantly & radically subverts the Western "law of genre" & moves nomadically between poem, novel & play, the latter genres being but ways of extracting specific moments of the writing. These extractions are all to often not based so much on the writer's own conceptions—even if the diasporic writer's struggles with or against those semi-foreign genres play a role, often positive but at times also limiting—but are more often imposed by the contingencies of the diasporic situation, in this case the French publishers' insistence for books circumscribed in ways that make the foreign text "readable" to a European audience.

This question—better: this problem—of genre will come up again & more radically so in an investigation of contemporary Maghrebian poetry & its nomadic wanderings between North & South. But before addressing the question of Arabic poetry, let us first look at how the North has done its best to occult the Arab roots of poetry in their domains, from Ezra Pound to Jacques Roubaud: the need to locate an indigenous, autochthonous origin of western poetry lead to the northern Mediterranean, Provence & the troubadours. As Maria Rosa Menocal recounted the story in a recent book, the field of romance philology (as well as the above mentioned poets) has done everything in its power to negate an Arab origin or even a strong originary influence on what it postulated as the origin of the European lyric. Open your American Heritage dictionary & the etymological root for the word *troubadour* will be given as a reconstructed, presumed & unattested (i.e. *) Latin root "tropare." And yet it has been known since at least 1928 (through the work of Julián Ribera), that the obvious root is the Arabic word "taraba," "to sing," & sing poetry; "tarab" means ecstatic song. Ezra Pound too was looking for euro-origins of lyric poetry, even if in his 1913 essay on the Troubadours he concedes a vague possibility as far as the tunes of their canzos are concerned: "They are perhaps a little oriental in feeling, & it is likely that the spirit of Sufism is not wholly absent from their content." And in the essay on Arnaut Daniel he writes:

> And he may, in the ending 'piula,' have had in mind some sort of Arabic singing, for he knew well letters, in Langue d'Oc & in Latin....So it is like as not he knew Arabic music, & perhaps had heard, if he understood not the meaning, some song in rough Saxon letters.

And that's it: once EP has established the origins of Euro-poetry in the canzone, its transformation & perfection by Dante, he is ready to move to China & Japan. Clarity was to be found only in the North, either the Asian one, or the Mediterranean one; the Mediterranean south is dismissed in one 1932 footnote from *Spirit of Romance*: "1932: Spanish point of honor, romanticism of 1830, *Crime passionel*, down to sardou & the 90's, all date from the barbarian invasion, African & oriental inflow on Mediterranean clarity."

Thus the Western refusal, century-long, to connect the Mediterranean, to open up to the Arabic, to envisage our lyric as also a diasporic entity. An entry, I think, maybe possible now via the work—mainly in French—of young post-independence Maghrebian writers. Their French is new, crisp, mestizo'ed, a "langue or littérature mineure" (as Gilles Deleuze & Félix Guattari propose in relation to Franz Kafka). Sitting in the weirdly named "Hôtel Transatlantique" (an old colonial French hotel chain, its name unchanged after independence & despite the fact that this desert place was a few thousand miles from the Atlantic ocean) in El Oued, the "Village of a Thousand Domes," an oasis of the Souf in the North-eastern corner of the Algerian Sahara, in 1977, I read Abdelwahab Meddeb's first book, *Talismano*, just received from his publisher Christian Bourgois in Paris. The newness of the book was instantly clear to me: no longer a novel, not a poem per se, but a autobio-narrative cum essay cum poetic perambulation of the mediterranean North & South, it may be best to call it a *récit*, a recital—in Blanchot's sense of the *récit* as non-novel, & in reference to the concept of the "recital" as the name for the Arabic narratives of Sufi mystics like Shorawardi (whom Meddeb has translated) or Ibn Arabi. The incredible thirty page opening description of immersion in the meanders of the medina of Tunis firmly sets the autobiographical origin as son of an Arab scholar & denizen of one of the oldest urban centers of commerce & learning of the Maghreb (reaching back to pre-Carthaginian times). One could even see in it a post-modern version of that traditional opening gambit of the classical pre-Islamic Arab ode, the *atlal*, already mentioned, in which the wandering poet returns & stops at the site of an old camp, & laments the ruins. But both content & form of what follows seem to immediately belie—or at least profoundly alter—such a supposed formal ghosting. For in *Talismano*, this opening section is followed—*instanter*, no cut, not even the seam of collage, but as rhizomatic offshoot—by a picnic in Venice on the tomb of EP, from whence the text will nomadize through France, Italy & Egypt, among other places.

Talismano is a paradigmatic text for a newer, post-independence, generation of Maghrebian authors. If the cultural confrontation that formed the basis of the elder generation's novels is still there as a theme, there is now a more complex consciousness of the bi- or multi-lingual diasporic space that subtends the writing. In that sense Meddeb's work can be seen as developing & practicing a theory of writing commensurate with the post-colonial diasporic situation & one that takes into account both the oral & the scriptural aspects of the Arabic language that ghosts the French text. For here, & maybe for the first time, Arabic ghosts the text not as some originary but lost—voluntarily or involuntarily—mother-tongue that has become unavailable or wants to be(come) unavailable in order to prove or help achieve the post-colonial modernity of the author through its overt rejection. It is there neither as *Verfremdungseffect* nor as orientalising ornament or realistic anchoring of the place, as is often the case in the more naively representational novel. It is there—or rather, its absence-presence works as a consciously thought through & acknowledged relationship to the other language, as witness, worker, energizer, transformer of the diasporic language in which the text presents itself. It is its live/hidden counterpart, set in motion by the writer in order to work through the diasporicity of his situation. His writing is thus indeed a *textum*, a weaving of the visible thread of the French & the invisible thread of Arabic—& it is the interweaving of both in a conscious & active engagement with the two languages that creates the final text, a true *amour bi-lingue* to use Abdelkebir Khatibi phrase.

But Arabic is not only another language at the levels of vocabulary, grammar, syntax, etcetera. It is also other in its scripturality, through which it connects to a core Arab art, calligraphy, involving both work on & extension of the act of writing, & which both obeys & circumvents the Qur'anic proscription of the representational. Here is how Meddeb himself formulates his position: "Comment peut donc écrire celui qui à l'origine calligraphie, puis travaille la langue qui, au depart, fascine parce que maîtresse de ce qui semble être chimérique puissance? [How then should he write who to begin with "calligraphs," then works (in) this language which fascinates to begin with, because mistress of what seems a chimerical power?"] In relation to *Talismano*, the critic Dina Al Kassim speaks of a "transgraphing" which she defines as a practice that "shifts the emphasis from a concern with semantic meanings toward a search for new terms & new forms of writing," in the process relocating "the ideological impasses of the national imaginary within the unraveling contexts of the linguistic, historical & religious complexity of Maghrebin culture." Meddeb himself speaks of this writing as "allography"—a writing that retools French—not by simply allowing Arabic words in, but by refiguring it at the grammatical & syntactical level (something that the reader experiences very strongly as a violence done to the language, especially as French is one of the most recalcitrant languages when it comes to such wrenchings). In order to analyze the work done by Meddeb's allographical poetics on a deeper level than the purely bi-lingual argument of an irreducible encounter between an "unwritable" because oral "mother tongue" & another form of standardized language, Al Kassim coins the very useful term "calligraphesis," a concept that "contains within itself both the specificity of meaning & the excess of its own staging." That calligraphy cannot be "translated" into the writing, she sees as

> the seeming limit [that] becomes for *Talismano* the scene of writing's promise as calligraphesis restores the problem of embodied meaning to the aspirations & proscriptions of the nation state embodied there. Far from being an ancillary effect, the illegibility of the calligraphic line is interior to legibility itself. The obvious & the obscure, the clear speech of state dictum & the unspeakability thus legislated, are intertwined in any writing that will acknowledge the calligraphic character of its own inscription.

Such an analysis also immediately points to the immense problems of translating works of this order into a further level of textual diasporal removal—into English, say. But it is also here that I see a major challenge for our own US-based avant-garde practice. For one, work such as Meddeb's & Tengour's (of whom more above[8]) seems to me to be much more boundary-breaking & challenging than most of the Parisian so-called avant-garde writing (despite notable exceptions, such as Pierre Guyotat's profound dislocation & re-inscription of an oral component into a French language that for most practitioners—even those as writerly avant-gardists as say, Michel Deguy or Jacques Roubaud or Pierre Alféri—remains based on the classical & profoundly static model of French). All too often—& despite valuable translations that are its outcome—the engagement of US avant-gardistas with French experimental writing, rather then being a diasporic displacement, turns out to be a recognition of sameness—& vice-versa. (An interesting example of this in relation to the novel is the tremendously positive French reception of Paul Auster's work, acclaiming it as the quintessential contemporary American novel, while seemingly blind to the fact that the "readability" of those novels *for the French* may well be premised on the Austerian text being ghosted by specifically Blanchotian & other post-structuralist French concerns).

(...)

But let me conclude by returning to the far western part of the world we have been engaged with, the Maghreb, which means the West, the Occident in Arabic & by quoting the Moroccan writer Abdelkebir Khatibi, from his book *Love in Two Languages:*

> Yes, I spoke, I grew up around the Only One & the Name, & the Book of my invisible god should have ended

---

[8] originally "below" as this essay continued with the core text of my introduction to the Habib Tengour Reader, which you can now read above, pp. xxx

within me. Extravagant second thought that stays with me always. The idea imposes itself as I write it: every language should be bi-lingual! The asymmetry of body & language, of speech & writing—at the threshold of the untranslatable.

Which leads Khatibi to say in another essay that what would indeed be extraordinary would be to write "à plusieurs mains, à plusieurs langues dans un texte qui ne soit qu'une perpétuelle traduction"—to write with/in several languages a text that would be but a perpetual translation. Isn't this exactly what those younger Maghrebian writers—Meddeb, Tengour & others discussed in this book—have been doing all along?

Resources:
Dina Al Kassim, "The Faded Bond:Calligraphesis & Kinship in Abdelwahab Meddeb's Talismano," *Public Culture, 13* (1), n.p. Available at: http://www.uchicago.edu/research/jnl-pub-cult/current/al-kassim.htm

Anonymous article in *L'Opinion*, available at: http://www.lopinion.ma/article.php3?id_article=1865

Driss Chraïbi, Le Passé Simple, Editions Denoël, 1954.

Jacques Derrida, *Monolingualism of the Other or the Prosthesis of Origin*, translated by Patrick Mensah, Stanford University press 1998.

Pierre Joris, *4X1: Works by Rainer Maria Rilke, Tristan Tzara, Jean-Pierre Duprey & Habib Tengour*, Inconundrum Press, 2002.

Abdelkebir Khatibi, *Love in Two Languages*, translation by Richard Howard, University of Minnesota Press 1990.

Abdelfattah Kilito, *Les séances: récits et codes culturels chez Hamadhani et Harîrî*, Paris, Sindbad, 1983.

Also now available in English by Abdelfattah Kilito:
Though Shalt Not Speak My Language (translated from Arabic by Waïl S. Hassan), Syracuse University Press, 2008.
The Clash of Images (translated from the french by Robyn Creswell), New Directions, 2010.
The Author & His Double (Essays on Classical Arabic Culture), translated by Michael Cooperson, Syracuse University Press, 2001.

Abelwahad Meddeb, *Talismano*, Sindbad, Paris 1987; English translation by Jane Kuntz, Dalkey Archives 2011.

Maria Rosa Menocal, *Shards of Love-Exile and the Origins of the Lyric*, Duke University Press, 1994.

Stefania Pandolfo, "The Thin Line of Modernity in some Moroccan Debates on Subjectivity". *In* Questions of Modernity, eds. T. Mitchell & L. Abu-Lughod. The University of Minnesota Press 2000.

Ezra Pound, *Literary Essays*, New Directions 1968.
_____. The Spirit of Romance, New Directions 1952.

(Paper given at the "Diasporic Avant-Gardes" conference held at the University of California, Irvine, 19-20 November 2004)

Touria Majdouline (Settat 1960)

A MINUTE'S SPEECH

To Oujda

The heart of Oujda is of stone,
Its hands a volcano and a wind,
And has no time for speech.

***

Here life passed me by
Here it passed
Leaving me in your weary arms
Striking the gates of silence,
O city of death,
Hoping that you open a door to dialogue
So can you spare some time for speech?

***

Your silence is exhausting
The choke became heavier
The bridge—to you—longer
So may I leave
Or can you spare
Some time
For speech?

***

You are a vertigo
With neither beginning
Nor end.
Come on stop a little while
I have a lot to say to you:
Air is all dust here
And life in you is like catching a cold.
So, could the world change tomorrow?
Could silence & gloom vanish?

***

you are a gate
opening onto another gate
A wall . . . a wall . . .
And a wall,
And I have for years
Been searching inside you
For a place
and for speech . . .

OUT OF CONTEXT

   I gather my confusion & my things
My steps
And the remaining illusions
Of my body
I run beyond time
Beyond the vacant air
And space

***

Yesterday I drew my open space here
And dreamed a lot
I sowed shade, & fruit, & crops around
And with flames I wrote my poems . . .
Yesterday
I had plenty of time
To embroider space with words.
But today
I am left with nothing
But my dejection
And the crumbs of yesterdays gone by

Thus I gather my things
I wrap myself up in my own confusion
And I run
I run beyond time
I propagate into the distance
With neither shade
Nor sun.

COMMENTARY

(1) Touria Majdouline, born 1960 in Settat, lives in Oujda where she teaches Arabic. Poetry International Web characterizes her work as follows: "The peculiarity of her poetry resides in its unpretentious style, which thrives on simple but skillful representations of reality. Her tone is quiet & discreet, but hides a remarkable bravery & boldness underneath. The speakers in her poems display a certain weariness of being, that is reminiscent in some ways of the poetry of reclusive American poet Emily Dickinson—although Majdouline's attitude to social life is very different. She is a highly active social co-worker, & president of the important Albadil Alijtimai association ('the social alternative'), which promotes the integration of children & young people into Morocco's social & cultural milieu. She is also a member of the union of Moroccan writers, the House of Poetry in Morocco, & a founding member of the UNESCO association for creative women of the Mediterranean."

(2) She has 3 books to date: *Uaraqu Arramad* (*Leaves of Ashes*), The Union of Moroccan Writers Publications, Rabat 1990; *al-Mut'aboon (The Weary)* by Dar al Jusoor, Oujda, 2000, & *Sama'un tushbihuni Qalilan* (*A Heaven which Somewhat Resembles Me*) in 2005.

Translated by Abdellah Benlamine & Norddine Zouitni

Introduction to *Diwan Ifrikiya*, a.k.a *The University of California Book of North African LiteRature*

This book has been incubating in our minds for a quarter century now, & we have been gathering material for even longer—with the aim of assembling & contextualizing a wide range of writing from North Africa previously unavailable in the English-speaking world. The result is, we believe, a rich if obviously not full dossier of primary materials of interest not only to scholars of world literature, specialists in the fields of Arab & Berber studies, but also to a general audience & to contemporary readers & practitioners of poetry who, to detourn a Frank O'Hara line, want "to see what the poets in North Africa are doing these days." It is a project meant as a contribution to the ongoing reassessment of both the literary & cultural studies fields in our global, postcolonial age. Its documentary & trans-genre orientation means that it not only features major authors & literary touchstones but also provides a first look at a wide range of popular cultural genres, from ancient riddles, pictographs, & magic formulas to contemporary popular tales & songs, & is also in part a work of ethnopoetics. Drawing on primary resources that remain little known & difficult of access, & informed by the latest scholarship, this gathering of texts illuminates the distinctively internationalist spirit typified by North African culture through its many permutations.

A combination of traditional & experimental literary texts & ethnopoetic material, this fourth volume in the ongoing *Poems for the Millennium* series of anthologies is a natural progression from its predecessors. Jerome Rothenberg & Pierre Joris edited the first two volumes, which present worldwide experimental poetries of the twentieth century. Volume 3, as a historical "prequel," covers the new & experimental poetries of nineteenth-century Romanticism worldwide. This volume—which we have at times half-jokingly thought of as a "sidequel," for its southerly departure from Europe & North America, the series's main focus—is conceptually linked in its attempt to present the historical processes that led to the most innovative contemporary work. And the first two, core volumes in fact include—although in a minimal manner, of necessity—a few of the Maghrebian authors who are revolutionizing writing in their countries today. Those books also show the importance of oral literature in contemporary experimentation, a theme deepened & broadened in the volume at hand.

Throughout the years of work on this book, our shorthand working title was "Diwan Ifrikiya," which has the advantage of being brief & concise, though the disadvantage of being slightly obscure compared to the longer, less elegant, but more explicit appellation *Book of North African Literature*. "Diwan Ifrikiya"—as we refer to it throughout this introduction—combines the well-known Arabic word for "a gathering, a collection or anthology" of poems, diwan, with one of the earliest names of (at least part of) the region that this book covers. Ifrikiya is an Arabization of the Latin word Africa—which the Romans took from the Egyptians, who spoke of "the land of the Ifri," referring to the original inhabitants of North Africa. The Romans called these people Berbers, but they call themselves the Amazigh, & even today tribal names—such as Beni Ifren—in their language, Tamazight, include words derived from *ifri*.

"Diwan Ifrikiya" is thus an anthology of the various & varied written & oral literatures of North Africa, the region known as the Maghreb, traditionally described as situated between the Siwa Oasis to the east (in fact, inside the borders of Egypt) & the Atlantic Ocean to the west, spanning the modern nation-states of Libya, Tunisia, Algeria, & Morocco—as well as the desert space of the Sahara. Given the nomadic habits of the Tuareg tribes, the larger Maghreb can include parts of Mali, Niger, & Chad, plus Mauritania, to the great desert's southwest, famous for its manuscript collections. (The spread of the various Amazigh peoples is also describable in terms of their basic food, namely the breadth & limits of the use of rolled barley & wheat flour, or couscous.) We have also included the extremely rich & influential Arab-Berber & Jewish literary culture of al-Andalus, which flourished in Spain between the ninth & fifteenth centuries. This culture was intimately linked to North Africa throughout its existence & even after its final disappearance following the Reconquista, given that a great part of Spain's Muslim & Jewish population fled toward the south then, seeking refuge in North Africa.

The time span of "Diwan Ifrikiya" reaches from the earliest inscriptions—prehistoric rock drawings in the Tassili & Hoggar regions in the southern Sahara; the first Berber pictograms—to the work of the current generation of postindependence & diasporic writers. Such a chronology takes in diverse cultures, including Amazigh, Vandal, Arab, Ottoman, & French constituents. It also covers a range of literary genres: although concentrating on oral & written poetry & narratives, especially those which invent new or renew preexisting literary traditions, our gathering also draws on historical & geographical treatises, philosophical & esoteric traditions & genres, song lyrics, current prose experiments in the novel & short story, & so forth.

From a wider or outside perspective, the overall chronological arrangement makes perceptible the crucial importance of this region in the development of Western culture, adding hitherto little-known or unknown historical data while showing how the Maghreb's present-day postcolonial achievements are major contributions to global world culture. In ancient times, the Maghreb was seen as the Roman Empire's breadbasket—we hope this book shows that at the intellectual & artistic levels this has remained so ever since. To be candid: North Africa is a region whose cultural achievements—including their impact on & importance for Western culture—have been not only passively neglected but often actively "disappeared" or written out of the record. This is true for the majority of this area's autochthonous writers & thinkers, even those few whose achievements have been recognized north of the Mediterranean—often because they became diaspora figures working in Europe. A few examples may suffice: Augustine is certainly considered a major church father, but his North African roots, if not totally obscured, are given little credit. Apuleius, the author of one of the first prose narratives that prefigure our novel, is known as a Latin or late Roman writer, not a Maghrebian. It is also interesting to note in this context that the last poet whose mother tongue was Latin was a Carthaginian, & that by an odd circumstance the first nonoral poet in our chronology, Callimachus—whose forebears immigrated to Cyrenaica (Libya), possibly from the Greek island of Thera, where the first ruler of the Battiad Dynasty came from—wrote in Greek.

We know that during the heyday of Arab-Islamic culture, & more specifically between 1100 & 1300 c.e., scribes & thinkers first safeguarded, then translated & transmitted to the Europeans, much of the Greek philosophy & science that we pride ourselves on as the roots of Western civilization. Many lived & worked in al-Andalus, that thriving center of culture on European shores—a place where a millennium ago Arabs, Jews, & Christians learned to live together in productive peace. Yet the core figures of this period of Arab culture, such as Ibn Khaldun, Ibn Battuta, & Al-Hasan Ibn Muhammad al-Wazzan al-Fasi—whom we know as Leo Africanus—if not unknown, are seriously marginalized in the West. Lip service may be paid to, say, Ibn Khaldun, as the father of sociology, or a French author of Lebanese origin may write a successful novel based on the figure of Leo Africanus, but the actual texts of these writers, thinkers, & mapmakers are rarely available to the Anglophone world—or are available only to specialists or, again, without much context with which to read & appreciate them.

Even if Arab culture went into a long sleep & the high-cultural productions of the Maghreb often became mere imitations of the classical Mashreqi (Near Eastern) models—and thus less creatively innovative—during the centuries between the fall of al-Andalus to the Spanish Christians & the conquest of North Africa by the colonial powers, there was much cultural activity then. This is especially true for the autochthonous Berber cultures which, despite having been Arabized (at least to the degree of accepting Islam, in many instances in a modified, maraboutic form), kept alive vital modes of popular oral literature, for example Berber tales & stories, plus elaborations & updated versions of the Arab-Berber epic of the Banu Hillal confederation. European anthropologists gathered much of this ethnopoetic material in the nineteenth & early twentieth century, but it has since faded from view, we surmise both from a lack of interest shown by the old colonizers & from a justifiable & understandable unease among Maghrebians toward this material so often labeled "primitive" or "preliterary" by those who recorded it. Besides which, the current Maghrebian societies are too busy trying to invent their own contemporaneity & to modernize themselves to have much time or desire to invest their limited resources in reassessing their remote pasts. If this anthology helps to dispel some of this unease or even incites other researchers & writers to look deeper into these hidden & buried histories, it will have accomplished one of its main goals.

The longtime neglect of such a major cultural area is part of a wider, now well-documented, Eurocentrism; permit us to cite an example germane to the project at hand. In the early days of Modernism, Ezra Pound spent time & energy establishing the roots of European lyric poetry, which he located in the French/Occitan troubadour tradition, a lineage that has become canonical over the past century. Open your American Heritage Dictionary, & you'll see that it gives the Latin tropare as the root of troubadour—an etymology that on closer inspection, however, turns out to be reconstructed, presumed, & unattested (i.e., marked with an asterisk). In fact, the field of romance philology has done everything in its power to negate any traces of a non-European origin of—or even strong foreign influence on—European lyric poetry. And yet it has been known since at least 1928, via the work of the Spanish linguist Julián Ribera, that the obvious root of troubadour is the Arabic tarab, "to sing," specifically to sing a musical poetry that produces an exalted state. (One could also link this ecstatic sense of tarab to Federico García Lorca's duende.) Pound, like nearly all other European & American writers & researchers, was looking for European origins—though in his 1913 essay on the troubadours he had a vague inkling that something else was going on, as far as the tunes of the troubadours' canzos are concerned: "They are perhaps a little Oriental in feeling, & it is likely that the spirit of Sufism is not wholly absent from their content." It is that kind of belittling and, in the final analysis, deeply denigrating attitude that "Diwan Ifrikiya" addresses and, we hope, redresses somewhat.

This anthology is organized into five approximately chronological diwans, inside which the authors appear in chronological order. Reading through them, one can get a sense of temporal progression & thus of the changes brought by history. The First Diwan, subtitled "A Book of In-Betweens: Al-Andalus, Sicily, the Maghreb," starts with an early, anonymous muwashshaha—that lyrical poetic form invented in al-Andalus which moved Arabic poetry away from the imitation of classical qasida models going back to pre-Islamic forms. After a wide presentation of Arab & Jewish poets who made al-Andalus so incredible & possibly unique, the diwan ends with Ibn Zamrak's wonderful description of the Alhambra.

The next diwan, "Al Adab: The Invention of Prose," presents a range of materials—from literary criticism through Ibn Khaldun's writings (the ur-texts of what will become sociology) to historical, literary, & cultural documents—that will give the reader a sense of the breadth & width of this pulsating & formative civilization. The Third Diwan, "The Long Sleep & the Slow Awakening," moves us from the end of the fifteenth century (and thus the end of al-Andalus, which can be dated to the final victory of the Spanish Reconquista, in 1492) to the end of the nineteenth, a period during which Arab culture—both in its cradle, the Middle East, & in its Western extension, the Maghreb (in fact, in Arabic Maghreb means "West," in both a geographical & a deeper cultural, even mystical, sense)—fell prey to what is usually called decadence, at the political, social, & cultural levels. For the Maghreb, however, even these centuries held creative excitement: it was then that one of the great poetic forms of North Africa, the melhun, came into its own by revitalizing its classical roots through both formal & linguistic innovations, including the use of the Maghrebian vernacular. The innovations & final grandeur of these poems, song lyrics really, are difficult to bring across in translation; suffice it to say that the poems have stood the test of time & still represent the core repertoire of the great melhun singers.

The Fourth Diwan, "Resistance & Road to Independence," covers about one hundred years: from the mid-nineteenth (the aftermath of the French colonization of Algeria) to the mid-twentieth century, that moment when the people of the Maghreb begin to demand—and fight for—sovereignty. The shock of colonization may at first have numbed these populations, but in the twentieth century they produced a literature of resistance while on what we have called the long road to independence. A specifically national or nationalist thought also emerged then, as a range of differences—between, before all, Tunisia, Algeria, & Morocco—rose to the surface & began to be theorized. Emblematic of this period are the diwan's two framing figures: Emir Abd El Kader, born in Mascara in 1808, the great nomad warrior who gathered the tribes to fight the French, was a superb writer & poet, & Sufi mystic, & a follower of Ibn Arabi's thought, who died in exile in Damascus; & Henri Kréa, the French-Algerian poet who fought for Algeria's independence & died in Paris in 2000. An amazing span—with other amazing figures, such as Abu al-Qasim al-Shabi, Frantz Fanon, & Kateb Yacine, whose work includes some of the first great classics of modern Maghrebian literature.

A double diwan concludes the book: although it covers only the past sixty or so years, its size demanded the split into two sections. We have divided it according to geography, grouping the two northeastern Maghreb countries (Libya & Tunisia) with the two relatively small countries in the south- west of our area, namely, Mauritania & Western Sahara, while keeping Algeria & Morocco for part 2. The writers in this diwan are those who came of age at the moment of independence & the two to three generations since then. This diwan's size & literary achievement show that the great richness that characterized early Maghrebian culture, even if buried for a time by the "decadence" of one of its foundational cultures & then by the strictures of European colonial impositions, has burst to the fore again—with a vengeance. This richness brings to mind the days of multicultural al-Andalus, even if today we would call it multinational or hybrid or cross-border. For instance, the youngest poet in the last—the Morocco—section of the book, Omar Berrada, sets his work presented here in the company of the three international figures whom he honors: the late-nineteenth-century French avant-gardist Alfred Jarry, the twentieth-century North American performance poet bpNichol, & the great Sufi poet & mystic Ibn Arabi (1165–1240), whom we will meet on several occasions throughout "Diwan Ifrikiya."

The diwans are interrupted, leavened, given breathing room—however you experience it—by a series of smaller sections, four "Books" & three "Oral Traditions," whose roles are multiple: filling in detail, giving context, or foregrounding specific areas. Thus "A Book of Multiple Beginnings" precedes the First Diwan, taking the reader from an early Berber inscription (see p. 10) to prehistoric rock drawings in the southern Sahara's Tassili & Hoggar regions through the first centuries of recorded literary output.

The Phoenician, Greek, & Roman writings from this period include some of the world-class achievements of Maghrebian culture.

Creation myths & tales of origin logically open this section. This puts the autochthonous Berber peoples rightfully at the start of the Maghrebian adventure while also foregrounding a tradition—the oral tradition—that has consistently produced major literary achievements over several millennia. This tradition is so ample & important that we had to create three independent sections ("Oral Traditions 1–3") dispersed throughout the anthology to try to do justice to its richness—which persists today, as the third of the sections, presenting contemporary oral work, shows. The distribution of these sections also reflects the fact that many of this anthology's contemporary writers source & resource themselves in that oral tradition's imaginary—one could go so far as to consider it the Maghrebian collective unconscious.

The other books concentrate on the poetry of the Sufi mystics ("A Book of Mystics"), on the very specific poetics of Arabic calligraphy ("A Book of Writing")—a core sense-making, meditative, & aesthetic dimension of Arab culture—and, finally, on a few diasporic writers ("A Book of Exiles"), both those who have left North Africa for whatever reason but feel them- selves Maghrebian despite their exilic position & those who have come & stayed, deciding to become Maghrebian or return to lost roots. Ironically, this smallest of subsections could be the largest: the diasporic or exilic dimension is one of the main characteristics of Maghrebian literature, given that the majority of its authors live & write on two or more shores.

Although it may seem counterintuitive for "A Book of Exiles" to include such writers as Hélène Cixous & Jacques Derrida, who are seen as essentially French (even if some of their work points to—and their late work indeed insists more & more on—the importance of their Maghrebian roots), their contributions here deal exactly with exile from the Maghreb & the related question of choice of language (see, for example, Derrida's essay *The Monolingualism of the Other*, which is a response to & an elaboration of the Moroccan poet & thinker Abdelkebir Khatibi's writings on this problem). Their work also helps to contextualize the problems of the surrounding obviously Maghrebian contemporary writers, who faced both the necessity of actual exile & the difficult decision of which language to write in. Although their mother tongue was usually one of several Berber languages or a *darija* (dialectal) variation of Arabic, more often than not they forwent these in favor of either the old colonial language, namely, French, or classical Arabic (which some Berbers, including even the great Algerian writer Kateb Yacine, consider as much of a colonial/imperial imposition as French).

Writing in French invariably connects the author with the old colonial metropole—no matter if he or she lives in the Maghreb or in self-imposed or forced exile elsewhere—as that's where the major publishing houses are (only recently have independent houses emerged in the Maghreb). Writing in Arabic means dealing with small local publishers & getting caught up in all the political & censorship problems this has meant for most of the time since independence, or trying to publish in Lebanon or Egypt, the major Mashreqi publishing centers. The latter is also fraught with problems, as Maghrebian & Mashreqian cultures do not necessarily coexist easily. But no matter if they publish in Paris or Beirut, these writers have little chance of being translated into & published in English. The little interest & financial support our cultural institutions & publishers have been able to garner for translations from French & Arabic have been squarely devoted to Parisian, Beiruti, & Cairene authors. Even greater are the difficulties of those Maghrebian authors who chose to write in Berber—though Morocco & Algeria have each recently declared it an official national language—or use the ancient tifinagh alphabet, as does the Tuareg poet Hawad, who now lives in southern France. It is therefore also an aim of this gathering to provide a space for the mixing & mingling (at least in

English) of writers who in their own countries & in other (usually country- or language-specific) anthologies have to exist in a kind of de facto cultural apartheid.

 Many if not most of the texts are appearing for the first time in English translation, while others are retranslations into contemporary American English of older Englished versions. The genres & the original languages—Tamazight (Berber), Greek, Latin, Arabic, & French—are manifold. Obviously a work of this order cannot be the work of one or even two persons. If we are the "author-editors" and, for some part, the translators of this anthology, we are fully aware of our limits: although between us we do have English, Latin, French, & Arabic, we do not know all the ages, all the languages, all the cultures that have contributed to this gathering. Our role has been threefold: (1) as the principal gatherers & arrangers of materials worked on by many other scholars, writers, & translators, (2) as the creators of the specific shape this book has taken (although here we owe a debt to Jerome Rothenberg, the collaborator with one of us on the first two volumes in the *Poems for the Millennium* series), & (3) as the purveyors of a range of translations done singly or in collaboration whenever no translations could be found, as well as of most of the contextual materials, such as prologues & commentaries, given to make more tangible & understandable the textual productions—poems, narratives, mystical visions, travel writings—of an area of the world not necessarily familiar to the general reader. To keep the volume from being overlong & to maintain focus on the texts themselves, we have not provided an individual commentary for every author although in many cases further information is included in the prologues. We do know the Maghreb well: Habib Tengour is Algerian, was born & raised in Algeria, taught at the University of Constantine for many years, and, though now based in Paris, returns to his home country & other Maghrebian countries a number of times a year. Pierre Joris also taught for three years in the 1970s at the University of Constantine (where he & Tengour met)

& has since returned regularly to this book's three core countries: Morocco, Algeria, & Tunisia.

It is our contention that "Diwan Ifrikiya" is especially important today, at a moment in history when the West's, especially the United States', convulsive engagement with Arab culture is in such a disastrous deadlock. Paradoxically, the United States is publishing more books on Arab countries, regimes, economics, & politics than ever before, though nearly all of them concentrate on the negative & paranoia-creating aspects of "Islamic terrorism" & do their best to claim noncivilization status for the region they cover (by suggesting, for instance, that it suffers from a combination of "primitive," bloodthirsty religion & misuse of modern Euro-American technologies) or are written from similarly dismissive perspectives. Such works do not permit the reader to understand what deeply animates these populations, in truth so near to us yet always pushed back & occulted. A book concerned with Maghrebian cultural achievements, in fields such as literature & philosophy, allows us to share in this universe, which is part of ours, no matter how deeply repressed. Knowledge of the Maghreb is, we believe, essential in a world where a nomadic mind-set is crucial for understanding (or inventing) the new century—especially if we do not want to repeat some of the deadliest errors of the last.

It is a marvelous coincidence that although we first thought of this book a quarter century ago, we actually gathered & wrote it exactly when Tunisia & Libya saw the start of a revolution, called the Arab Spring, that is still going & may be the shape-shifter that will determine the outcome of this century. We hope that through its polyvalent view of the region's cultural achievements, our book will help to further a deeper understanding of this strategic part of the world.

Pierre Joris & Habib Tengour
New York / Paris Spring 2011

OUIDAD BENMOUSSA (QASR EL KEBIR, 1969)

RESTAURANT TUYETS

I love the morning of your heart
The night of your eyes
The cardinal points of your smile
...
...
...
The candle
Pricks up its ears to
Warmth
We could no longer offer
...
...
...
The candle awaits
The birth
Of a kiss...

THIS PLANET... OUR BED

This planet readied itself
For me to dwell in you
No ocean in my eyes
But waves
No spring in my hands but sound

I am created by a kiss
For me to dwell in you
Feeling my way along your shudders
As if we were sky and
Earth

...
...
This planet... our bed

ROAD OF CLOUDS

Until now your visions were unclear to me
Your horizon, too far to help
I follow your steps
Melt in your flawless crystal
Tell you the torment of my secrets
In
Passion
I name you:
My sister nomad
Oh cloud,
So distant

Translated by Emma Hayward

COMMENTARY

Born in 1969 in Ksar el Kebir in north-west Morocco, arabophone poet Ouidad Benmoussa's first collection, *The Imminent Root*, published in Rabat in 2001, established her as a poet to watch. Her second collection, *Between Two Clouds*, was published by Marsam, Rabat, in 2006 (selected poems published in Banipal 30, 2007). She is a member of the Board of the House of Poetry in Morocco, & writes for Morocco's *Al-Alam* newspaper. Selected poems have been published in French translation in Abdellatif Laâbi's anthology *La Poésie marocaine de l'Indépendence à nos jours* (2005), while other poems translated into English by Ali Issa are available in BANIPAL 35.

On Poetry & Miscegenation: Interview by Orlando Reade

Sorry for this extremely slow response to your last, thanks for agreeing to answer some questions. In the last week I've been working through the book, trying to work out how to ask the questions which will reflect what I admire so much about the anthology. So here goes:

1. The anthology includes a series of origin myths, & reflects an extraordinary array poetic relations between language & land. Could you tell us about the history of your friendship & collaboration with Habib, where & when you conceived the idea of the anthology?

Habib & I met in 1976 at the University of Constantine where I was teaching in the English Department & he in the Department of Sociology. We became friends when we discovered that we were both poets & had very similar interests. We stayed in touch over the years & would meet from time to time in Paris, where Habib moved in the 80s, when I'd come through that town.

I'd thought up the idea of the anthology even earlier—an ur-sense of the need for such a book came to me in 1966 when I met the Moroccan poet Mohamed Khaïr-Eddine in Paris & he introduced me to Maghrebi literature, insisting that it was in the Maghreb that the most interesting & revolutionary literature was happening. That's when I began to read widely in that literature (as well as in Caribbean francophone literature, as both of these felt richer & wilder & more alive than French "metropolitan" poetry).

Then, in the 80s when Jerome Rothenberg & I imagined & developed the concept of the *Poems for the Millennium* anthologies, I immediately thought that this concept could be expanded & that I could finally put together this volume on the Maghreb. It seemed useful, in fact, necessary to bring in another person to collaborate on the project, & Habib was a natural, as one of the most accomplished & experimental poets of the Maghreb & as an excellent scholar in the various areas of Maghrebi cultures (as a trained anthropologist, he is, for example a specialist of oral literatures). A year & a half later we handed in the ms.

2. Anthologia, from the Greek, is about a collection of flowers; flowers which are, presumably, dead. I wonder whether placing poems in an anthology always involves cutting them off from their roots, preserving them in a lifeless state. Translation redoubles this danger, removing the text from its source-language. So it seems that an anthology in translation poses a number of dangers to the life of a poem. Does the anthology form & the translation form preserve or alter the life of the poems in different ways? Is there a kind of death involved in this process?

The cut flower etymology is a bit of a dead metaphor. Any poem in any magazine or book could be considered a cut flower—i.e. where is the natural, organic garden habitat of the poem? The handwritten notebook, the hard disk on which it is preserved, the live reading? A poem is not a product of nature, it is an artifact. And that applies not only to written & printed, i.e. Gutenbergian artifacts, but also to the oral tradition—*Technicians of the Sacred* is what Jerome Rothenberg has called the poets in that tradition & they too create artifacts, word-constructs shaped with artificial techniques. Both of us think of the anthologies we have created—alone, together or with others—as "grand collages" to use Robert Duncan's lovely phrase. They are, like any poem, a multilayered construct. This does not mean that a poem does not change when its environment changes. A given poem in an anthology will be ever so slightly changed, inflected by the poems by other poets that surround it, than it is in its other "unnatural habitats"—but it is exactly this event, the fact that a new environment enriches a given poem, possibly reveals layers or shadings that had gone unperceived, that to me is proof of the continuing & expanding "life" (if we have to use that organic metaphor) of the poem.

And it is exactly at that level that our anthologies want to be different from the traditional, dead, pressed, preserved flower-anthology which are meant as morgues.

3.   This blog is often devoted to questions of geography & epistemology, in Africa & its diaspora. Readers of your anthology might be disappointed—surprised, more likely—that so much of its contents exceeds the borders of modern-day North Africa, towards Provence, Andalucia, Sicily, Iraq & Syria. If the anthology is a kind of nomadic institution, why devote it to a region rather than a specific language or dialect?

Like all live & lively cultures, maybe even more so, the culture of North Africa shows a diastole / systole contraction/ expansion rhythm over time. And so yes, there was a moment when the cultural area of the Maghreb included Spain, or at least Andalucia. That culture, usually referred to as al-Andalus, had its origins in the Middle East, but then formed & found its center in Spain, with its cultural goods, especially poetry becoming influential beyond the strict geographical borders of al-Andalus, &, so I argue, constituting the base from which troubadour poetry in Provence & beyond developed. Twice the North African Berbers were called to the rescue by their co-religionary brethren in Spain, & when al-Andalus finally was destroyed by the Spanish, many of its Muslim & Jewish citizens found refuge in the Maghreb. In Sicily it was the European court that thought so highly of the Al-Andalus /Arab culture that it invited people from there into its government & adopted its cultural mores. A great Murcia-born poet & Sufi teacher like Ibn Arabi would spend time in Fez (I was recently shown the little mosque, still standing, very lopsided, propped up by wooden boulders, waiting for UNESCO money for overdue repairs, where he worshipped in the Medina), go to Tunis, move on to Mecca (remember that the Hadj is one of the duties of all good Muslims) & wind up living & dying in Damascus. What interests me a lot is the nomadic openness of this culture—just compare the travels & travel diaries of Ibn Battuta to those of his European equivalents, say Marco Polo, & you'll see the difference in openness.

What interests me too is the diastole/systole of the region over time, complexified by the languages that nomadically come & go, *au gré du conquérant* over those two millennia & more. Had we had 300 more pages we would have investigated the southern borders of the regions in more detail, i.e. Tschad, Niger, Mali—Timbuktu alone could be a fat chapter or rather diwan—to look at the border complexities where the Saharan cultures meet the African ones. We got a little sample of that into the Mauritania & Western Sahara sections. So it is not the definition of a region by drawing borders, limits, but rather the expansiveness, or at least porousness of a border that interest me—what crosses over & mixes is more interesting than what tries to stay stubbornly "pure" or exclusive. As I've said elsewhere & keep repeating, miscegenation is the only way to advance, to make it new.

4. In the section, 'The Invention of Prose' you quote a description of Africa by Al-Hasan' Ibn Muhammad al Wazzan al-Fasi (a.k.a Leo Africanus): "In the Arabian tongue, Africa is called Ifrikiya, from the word Faraka, which in the language of that country means "to divide." The anthology is split up into five 'Diwans' & seven chapters, some of which are divided by country or region, & some by individual author. Is there anthology's work as making both division & connection between cultures?

Yes indeed, that is part of an anthology's work. To make the distinctions that will allow the connections to stand out the more clearly. I've always considered anthologies as networks that, while highlighting differences, create connections—be they between genres, authors, geographical or cultural realms—that will create a *textum*, i.e. a weave—in this case, permit me to orientalize a bit, a carpet, a flying one hopefully... I am not interested in the anthology as the alphabetically (or otherwise) arranged list of the cultural hit-parade, like "the hundred best poems in the X-language." Such anthologies always rely on an accredited (by/with what powers?) editor who promises "only the best." This approach itself has become a vitiated one given that a core move of 20C art & writings into the present has been the move away from the single, self-contained work that claims "masterpiece" status. "Master"—just think on that word & all it entails ideologically...

5. The volume is dedicated 'To those poets of the Maghreb & the Arab worlds who stood up against the prohibitions.' In your view, how has the so-called Arab Spring affected the demands for the translation of literature from North Africa? [i.e. are there texts, new or old, which we now need to have translated? are there texts which no longer look so urgent? How can literature help us to understand the Maghreb since 2011?]

This is a tough & complicated question or issue & one I'm not necessarily equipped to answer. But let me try to talk to this. The so-called Arab Spring was sparked by the first protests that occurred in Tunisia on 18 December 2010 in Sidi Bouzid following Mohamed Bouazizi's self-immolation. I read somewhere that to give the event a wider historical context one of the first TV reports quoted the Tunisian poet Abu Al-Qasim Ash-Shabi's "The Will of Life"—a work from the late 20s/early 30s, which we print in Christopher Middleton & Sargon Boulos' translation in the anthology.

This poem, as well as another one by Ash-Shabi, "To the Tyrants of the World," was quoted, chanted, sung, recited during the protests & marches in Tunisia, Egypt & beyond. We use, on purpose, not any of the available more literary or "poetic" translations of "To the Tyrants..." & which are in the main rather weak, but a decent prose rendering by Adel Iskandar, which NPR used while covering events on Tahrir Square .

We know the importance of modern media in the spread & the very tactics of the revolts, & I've often wondered in the first months of the uprising if Gil Scott Heron (who passed away in May 2011) —& who's also the guy who said "The first time I heard there was trouble in the Middle East, I thought they were talking about Pittsburgh"—was able to watch some of the events & reflect on his famous "The Revolution Will Not Be Televised." In that early seventies piece he meant that people had to get off their couches & take to the streets, & that is indeed what happened, but at the same time, the fact that Tunis & Tahir Square were televised 24/7 & that the new social media, handheld, was able to both set up tactical communications between the participants & feed the frenzied image need of that junky TV set in your living room, was how these events "made it new." Difficult to say if poetry "made it new" in relation to the Arab Spring, though obviously from Ash-Shabi to the current generation of poets, much of the thinking that needed to be done has been done there. The Maghreb as a multilayered cultural space with both strong oral & written media has worked toward a possible liberation, first from the colonizers & then from the illegitimate totalitarian regimes that followed & were abetted by the ex-colonizers, all through the 20C. From the lyrics of a singer like Cheikha Rimitti to the acidly critical poems of someone like Amin Khan, we can trace this work, these demands for change, these criticisms of a static petrified cultural & political situation. So the dedication of our book "To those poets of the Maghreb & the Arab worlds who stood up against the prohibitions" refers not only back to those who did this & were suppressed by their culture & governments—some, like Mouloud Feraoun or Tahar Djaout were killed, assassinated because they spoke out—but also to the present poets & artists who are doing this.

But your question had to do with how the so-called Arab Spring has affected the demand for translations from that part of the world. Not much if at all—at least in the field of poetry. Oh yes, there is a demand for non-fiction books on Arab & Muslim matters, there is even a slight up in demand for fiction (a good way to follow this is to check in on Marcy Lynx Qualey's site *Arab Literature (in Translation)*. Though the fact that demand for translations from those parts of the world is up, because of, first 9/11, then the Afghanistan & Iraq war, & now the so-called Arab Spring, should let us think carefully about this matter. I was talking about this in my 11/8 Brussels conference keynote, where I criticize the 'official' writing that has emerged from those circumstances & quote poet & translator Ammiel Alcalay, who said:

> How are those of us involved in transference & translation to respond to such circumstances? What is our role in the politics of imagination & transmission? *Have we reached a point where NOT translating, providing access to, handing down works from the Arab world might be more legitimate?* When we decide to participate, how do we insulate & protect such works & ourselves, not merely from assimilation, but from collaboration... Writers & translators often wind up playing someone else's game, & become complicit, perpetuating the same rules with new players. (emphasis mine)

Which leads Alcalay to conclude that no act of transmission is innocent & therefore demands utmost vigilance, a kind of vigilance, he goes on, "that recognizes, as the American poet Jack Spicer once put it, that 'there are bosses in poetry as well as in the industrial empire." We have to be aware that, for example, translating a major novel by an Arab (or other third) world author wrenches that work out of its natural habitat, plops it into an environment where it can only be read according to the latter's rules (say, Kateb Yacine's *Nedjma*, in relation to William Faulkner's narrative universe, etc.) Or, more viciously as in the case of my translation of Abdelwahab Meddeb's essay *The Malady of Islam* which was nearly hijacked by DC rightwing think tank people when Daniel Pipes asked the NY publisher for first serialization rights & the right to "subedit" the extracts—I managed to fight this off after a quick investigation.

So, more & more I think that given that the right solution, which would be to tell people to learn the language so they can read the books in the original, is impracticable & bound to fail, we need to keep translating—but that maybe we should change our habits, & realize that it is also the translator's duty to provide contextual materials, so as Ammiel puts it, "to protect against assimilation & collaboration," something that "requires more than fitting newly introduced & revived texts into existing frameworks. Defining what information is for us, where it comes from, & where to find it becomes an essential survival kit." An excellent example of this is the recent work of Madeleine Campbell (she just successfully completed a PhD on translating the Algerian poet & novelist Mohamed Dib at the University of Glasgow) who, besides translating a full book of poems by Dib, & writing some excellent essays on that process, also added writing which she calls "jetties" & that bring much needed contextual information on the author & his culture to the Euro-American reader via performance, readings, assemblages of quotes & other materials by the author & beyond, creating a matrix of relevant information allowing for a reading of the translated author's work on his or her own terms more than on the terms of the target culture. So yes, there is massive literary material that needs to be translated, & there is even more massive quantities of cultural materials that need to be made available.

Malika El Assimi (Marrakech, 1946)

SMOKE

The evenings suffocate me
and through me grow light
I switch on my sun
and its clarity overwhelms me
I pursue the winds
so that they extinguish my fire
and reduce me
to a body
of smoke

MARIAM

O you who gathers me
on this rainy night
like a radiant cherry
on the humid branch
You who walk between the branches
and caress me
I collapse between your hands
and you discover the ecstasy
the just law of this universe
They said:
Shake, o Mariam, the palm frond
so that the dates will fall for the children
And Mariam shook her father's palm tree
Adam
O you who shudder
when the wind blows on eyelashes

and makes stars tremble
if you knew
what a heart holds

THE SNOUT

Poetry will be your dress
when you yield your soul
back to its maker
You'll strike down your enemies
through mortal silence
and the language assassinated
under your fingers
With it you'll tattoo
the snout of the good-for-nothings
and you'll bring down the sphinx a peg or two

COMMENTARY

Malika al-Assimi, a poet, writer & teacher, also actively involved in politics, has fought discrimination against women, especially in public service, all of her life. Though she lost her first electoral bid to represent her Marrakech district in the Moroccan parliament, she won the seat on the second try. In the early 1970s she founded & published the journal *al-Ikhtiyar* (The Choice), & has contributed to other journals, such *al-Thaqafa al-Maghrebiyya* (Maghrebi Culture). Her poetry has always been strongly centered on empowering women in all aspects of their lives—socially, politically & culturally. As A. Laâbi writes: "Malika al-Assimi has played the role of outrider for [Moroccan] women, when one realizes that before her, poetry was a quasi male monopoly. Her contribution is all the more estimable as from the very start she took an offensive line. The stakes did not revolve about making a "feminine voice" heard, but were about inserting oneself naturally into the process of the poetic renaissance in progress. And to this process she brought something often lacking in the male voice: a different relation to the body, to the forces that manifest life or try to destroy it, including in the private sphere. In this rough male winter, it is through an interior sun that her poetry lights our way." Besides a number of volumes of poetry—including , *Kitabat Kharij* Aswar al-'Alam (1988, Writings Outside the Walls of the World), & *Aswat Hanjara Mayyita*(1989, Voices from a Dead Throat)—she has published a book dealing with political issues regarding women, *al-Mar'a wa Ishkaliyyat al-Dimuqratiyya* (Women & the Ambiguities of Democracy). And one on the history of Jam'i al-Fina, the famous square in Marrakech. Translated from Abdellatif Laâbi's French versions by P.J.

Postlude

As I read through the final proofs for this book in early March 2019, I keep getting interrupted by messages coming in via WhatsUp—it is old friend Habib Tengour whom the reader will have met on several occasions earlier in this book, sending photos & videos live from Algeria—& by my own compulsion for checking Al Jazeera TV or French radio as the news of the "ras-le-bol," the loud 'nuff-already of the Algerian people starts to boil over into the streets at the announcement of next month's "elections" — the government's attempt to make Abdelaziz Bouteflika, a sick old man right now hospitalized in Switzerland, puppet-president for the fifth time. I can't help checking Face Book & twitter threads & posting myself, and thus early on the 9th, I post this to FB:

> 'makach al khamssa ya Bouteflika' Wow! The demonstrations in Algeria are a breath of fresh air in the Maghreb. Women & children in the front rows. So far, so good. But the gangsters who have hijacked the country will not simply hand over the keys to the government (or to their bank-accounts into which the wealth of the country has been drained).

Later in the day I elaborated on this little text for a post on Nomadics blog as preface to a series of photos by Tengour, adding:

> ... It looks like the country has finally woken up from a long, long sleep. During what came to be called the 2011 "Arab Spring' in Tunisia, Morocco, Egypt, Libya, the "chape de plomb," the leaden weight (the expression

derives from a medieval instrument of torture) that lay over Algeria had kept the people of that country from revolting — although they had as many valid reasons to do so as the Tunisians or the Egyptians did.

But they were held back by their remembrances of the devastating civil war of the 90s that caused several hundred thousand deaths-by-assassination (indiscriminately perpetrated by islamists &/or the military) & that had followed the last attempt to democratize the country: in 1991 the first free-ish multi-party elections since independence were cancelled by a military coup after the first round when the military expressed concerns that the FIS, the Islamic Salvation Front, was almost certain to win more than the two-thirds majority of seats required to change the constitution & would thus be able to democratically form an Islamic state. The civil war lasted a decade, after which the same crew(s) & clans (with the help of the military & the FLN's single party formed after the end of the war of independence in 1962) came back to power.

Meanwhile via WhatsUp I have been in touch with Habib Tengour, the Algerian poet & novelist, who happens to be traveling in Algeria right now & happens to be in Constantine, the city we met in in 1976 when we were both teaching at the university there. Habib has been sending me the photos he takes as he walks the city among the citizens, men, women, children out on the streets, chanting: "Makach al khamssa ya Bouteflika—No Fifth for Bouteflika!

Then, on the morning of 10 March, I post another photo to Facebook with the following commentary: "Can't get Algeria out of my mind: a note during the night from Habib Tengour that a general strike has been proclaimed. This morning Nadia Ghanem (see my "Nomadics" blog) cites Prime Minister Ahmed Ouyahia who said on February 28 before the National Assembly, that protesters should remember what happened in Syria. But even when the people withdraw from the street, the pavement reveals (see picture) the demands: no 5th term for Bouteflika. The Algerian people—& the world—needs & deserves a successful revolution. Don't wish for it, don't pray for it—but work for it!"

"Tout est possible—everything is possible" says Nedjib Sidi Moussa on France Culture this morning, Monday march 11, while Adlène Meddi, on the phone from Algiers speaking on the young population of the country (70% are under 30) quotes someone else's as saying "These young people have not travelled but they have seen the world." Via internet is the inference, I believe, but also by being conscious of events in their & the wider Arab world, and the West: they are in the main trilingual, having Algerian Arabic, French, often some English & for many of them a Berber mother-tongue.

But what seems to drive most of them is finally a sense of humiliation: how the people of the country has been humiliated by their own supposedly "revolutionary" governments, in their material impoverishment (as one of the hand-held poster had it: "They have the millions, but we are the millions!") & in the loss of national self-esteem they sustain when seeing the world laugh or shake its head at a government proposing yet one more time the same "grabataire," the same bedridden mummy as the official presidential candidate.

What makes me somewhat upbeat about this popular uprising (I dislike the world "revolution" for its etymology which always sends the concept back to a "going around in circles" as do the cylinders of "revolvers") is something we have trouble getting our heads around in this country. There are two public spaces in Algeria where people can come together safely and express their opposition to the powers that be. The first is the mosque — & that's where in the 80s the fundamentalist Islamists had managed to convince a majority of young & older people to vote for their reactionary party in those first open elections held in 1989, which led to the 10-year civil war already mentioned. The second is the stadium, which, despite the fact that in the main only men frequent these public places, has been an amazing space where to built & feel pride in one's community & where to create songs & slogans to show one's defiance of the authoritarian government. Many of the slogans & songs heard these weeks in the streets of Algeria were first experimented with in the stadiums. As one young fan of the USM (the Union sportive de la medina d'Alger soccer club) put it to a journalist: "The songs give us real strength. In the stadium it's the political messages that make our anger and excitement rise the most, and they do the same for the police facing us, as they raise and fix their leg-protectors and tighten their grips on their clubs."

So these weekend sports occasions, traditionally & in almost all countries a way of channeling popular dissatisfaction *away* from political demands, have here proved to be a rehearsal space for a countrywide demand for change. A demand for change and for victory, not for one's local soccer club, but for one's image of a just, egalitarian & democratic country, a victory against the enemy within, that gerontocracy doing its best to bleed the country out.

*

I have to put this book to bed before the results of the Algerian uprising are known. Last night "the frame" — as Bouteflika is known given that only a framed photograph of his likeness is paraded around on official occasions, as he is wheelchair- &/or hospital-bound — made public a letter written for him by an unknown entity, committee or individual (his kid brother Said, most likely) exercising the actual power behind the scenes, stating that he would not seek a fifth term. This is good news, indicating that the people in the streets were heard & can't simply be ignored any longer. But more ominous was a second letter that stated that the elections were pushed back to the end of the year & that Bouteflika & his government would work at preparing the new constitution, giving himself thus an un-elected 8 or 9 months extra rule. The latest message from Habib Tengour, now in Algiers, was: "situation préoccupante." Translating that adjective describing the situation isn't easy; a number of words propose themselves & I'll cite them all, as they all fit: "disturbing *adj* · troubling *adj* · serious *adj* · disquieting *adj* ."

Will this peaceful revolution succeed? Will the old ones fold their hand of marked cards under popular pressure & move to their golden dachas or Swiss villas to live out their lives coddled by the immense bank accounts of stolen public moneys they have squirreled away? Or will their addiction to raw power & their greed make them send troops into the streets to open fire on the people? When this book comes out in a couple of months, we will no doubt know more.

I would like to close this postlude & thus *Arabia (not so) Deserta* with an excerpt from the Egyptian poet & film-maker Safaa Fathy's book *Revolution Goes Through Walls*, a collection of poems & texts I helped her translate into English a year ago & that celebrate the Tahrir Square uprising in Cairo during that country's 2011 "Arab Spring." May the current Algerian version come to a better conclusion! Salam.

Brooklyn, 11 March 2019

Safaa Fathy

from: *Revolution goes Through Walls*

SNAPSHOTS

- Tell your feet that don't want to go where you want to go that the journey is toward absence.

- When the gas entered my lungs I decided to start smoking again.

- The taxi driver took me as far as Al Abbassya and held his hand out to greet me. He and I are incidentals encountering each other in the space of a city, in 2011. He represented the Brothers and I, the others.

- We wore masks to protect ourselves from the gas. We knew perfectly well that they were signs to recognize our faces while we marched.

- On the Square an old man came toward me carrying a tray of "kushari." I said to him: in the new constitution women have to be given all their rights.

- When a young man's cold hand grabbed mine as I entered the Square through the Talaat Harb barricade, I yelled at him and he let me through without controlling my national identity card number.

- Each time I came through the Abdelmeneim Riad barricade, the young girl who body-searched me would say please forgive me, and I would forgive her immediately.

- I stood behind a sheikh who was sermonizing on Tahrir Square. Each time he said something beautiful, I'd add: well said! Then he would say even more beautiful words.

- Some men sat down on the sidewalk and wrote slogans on bits of cardboard. Exhausted, they wore the slogans on their heads like hats.

- I entered the sentry box of a traffic policeman in front of the Ministry of Foreign Affairs. A history Professor, originally from the Delta, already sat there, resting from a night spent standing, securing the Square.

- Each time I tried to photograph from on high, I took the place of some young man who helped me sit on top of the green barrier.

- The young man who left me enough space to put a foot down on the roof of the Tahrir subway station in order to watch the speech of the ousted one on the 10th of the second month of the year 11, yelled: he still uses the future tense! I told him: you have become a symbol!

- Two young men were listening to the speech of February 10, and their heads were so conjoined that I thought I was witnessing the emergence of a new human species.

- On the Square I saw old friends I hadn't seen for a very long time. Their eyes were bulging, red, their faces haggard. I understood that we had never met before.

- I hadn't thought it was a revolution until I heard a man of the people yell into his phone: I am not at a demonstration, I am in a revolution.

- I saw a young man with a white bandage over one eye when I entered the field hospital on the Square. There was a piece of banana by his side, and a young girl who's asked me: Where from?

- The night of the ouster I saw a blind young man carrying a tape recorder and a microphone. He was asking the passerby's for their feeling in order to see them.

- One evening the soldiers didn't want a young man to accompany me on Kasr el Nile bridge. I threatened them: if I get killed I'll come back to haunt you. Then they allowed him to accompany me.

- I learned how to hitch-hike in Cairo on the evening of January 28.

- On the evening of the Battle of the Camel, I was carefully proceeding toward Abdelmoneim Riadh Avenue. That's when I saw Nassif, my friend from Paris, in the process of throwing a brick. I said to him: lend me your shoulder so that I may rest my camera on it.

- The smallest van that ever gave me a lift came along on the 28th and was driven by a man with bulging red eyes behind lenses as thick as the bottom of the small tea glasses used in the Saïd (Upper Egypt).

- On the 28th I took the last taxi in Cairo when an old friend threw me out of his house in the middle of the night.

- My feet were in a different space-time when I saw the son of my oldest friend relish the sight of an armored vehicle crushing a man in Suez.

- An officer, a member of my family, took refuge with us. We suggested he bring his weapons along so that we may protect them.

- I had a dear friend I didn't see as I was moving about the Square. She was home in the process of transmitting the latest news to friends abroad.

- Heba was sitting on the floor at the office of Merit Publishers. She was writing articles for Al Ahram newspaper after having told her mother: I would like my son to be an orphan.

- I was speaking on the phone with the mother of a young girl crying because she wanted to stay on the Square; it took my breath away when the mother said: the Square is for men only.

- One evening my sister and I were leaving the Square when a group of doctors in white coats from Tahrir Square walking behind us said: don't stray, so that we may protect each other.

- One morning I woke up on an old carpet at the offices of Merit Publishers and I discovered a novelist sleeping right next to me.

- After the cell phones were stolen, I had to hide the camera in a kitchen utensil so that it could charge while I was sleeping.

- On the day of the Battle of the Camel we filled empty bottles with water and threw them into the street toward the demonstrators through a hole in the door of Merit publishers.

- On the day of the Battle of the Camel we turned the lights out, drew the black curtains shut and through a small circle Hachem had cleaned on the widow pane, I pointed my camera to record the Molotov cocktails exploding on Talaat Harb square.

- On the day of the Battle of the Camel, Manal distributed water bottles to those who were holding the line. One of them scolded her, telling her to go hide.

- As I crossed the Square under a hail of stones, a young man took me by the hand, took off his jacket and put it over my head.

- Crossing the Square I photographed a poor woman hard at work breaking tiles into projectiles. One hour later my film was stolen.

- Maybe what we lived through is enough. It is neither s step forward nor a step backward. But a step toward a road blocked by a small wall.

- When the men were folding the blankets to leave the Square I wished I had a big book the leaves of which I could have spread over them so that they wouldn't leave.

- Each time I asked a young man for help, I discovered that he was the son of an old comrade.

- Each time my sister Hala and I came back to the house at night, the people in the street welcomed us as if we were warriors on a 12 hour furlough.

- On the 28th I saw a man holding a little girl by the hand, her eyes reddened by the gas. Why did you put her in danger? It is she who brought me here.

- People spoke into my camera as if they were archiving their stories while sending messages to the world.

- Over toward the field hospital, on the night of the Battle of the Camel, there was a young boy with a wound to his head, who was taking care of himself all by himself.

- Every time I needed a shoulder to rest my camera on I found a man to whom I said: you are old, let me lean on you.

- On the evening of the ousting I stared into the face of the peasant woman who had sat in on the Square since day one; she sat alone in the darkness, weeping.

- Nizar Samek's sister wept and said that Nizar wished we would finally grab the thread by its true beginning.

- It is the first time I see the verb "to want" move the lips of all those present.

- Throughout these days I never saw Mohamed Sachem eat or sleep. He only talked and smoked.

- A few days later I walked in Al Muhandisin and I heard the road workers' yells — greeting the revolutionaries by greeting me.

- People came to the Square as if visiting relatives. Everyone carried a bag of food. As soon as they detected a sign of fatigue on someone's face, they would offer some food.

- Months later, walking along an alleyway in the center of town, I heard a young man singing under his breath, "Revolution, revolution until victory... in all of Egypt's streets."

- From the windows of Merit Publishers, day after day I photographed a group of young people in the process of building a catapult to throw stones.

- Two years later one of them became my faithful friend Ibrahim.

- As if we are not supposed to remember those days, do we have to say how naive we were, two years later?

- The young came with a freight hoist to tear down the gate of the Al Ittihadia palace but the army had grabbed the guide line. They exchanged one prisoner for five arrested revolutionaries, to be liberated at dawn. Maybe we are even more naive... to be continued.

Acknowledgements

"Arabic Poetics & the International Literary Scene," lecture delivered at Naropa University, September 19, 2001. *CROSS WORLDS: Transcultural Poetics* (An Anthology), Editors; Anne Waldman & Laura Wright, Coffee House in 2014.

"Homage to Mohammed Khaïr-Eddine," first published in Banipal no. 10/11 spring/summer 2001. Reprinted in *Justifying the Margins*, Salt Publishers, 2009.

"From Exile to Transgression: On Adonis," Introduction to Adonis poetry reading in N.Y. November 4, 2005. First published in *Justifying the Margins*, Salt Publishers, 2009.

"A Conversation in the Pyrenees" extracts from *A Conversation in the Pyrenees: Adonis with Pierre Joris*, Contra Mundum Press, 2018.

"Introduction To *Exile is my Trade: A Habib Tengour Reader*." Black Widow Press, *2011*.

"On Abdelwahab Meddeb" Banipal #52, 2015.

"Homage to Mohamed Bennis: A Shared Testament." Talk delivered at *Homage à Mohammed Bennis*, 38th International Cultural Moussem at Al Moutamid Ibn Abbad Summer University on July 19, 2016 in Assilah, Morocco.

"Prize Fights." New Statesman, 7 December 1979, London

"Introduction to *A Passenger from the West*." UNO Press, 2010.

"Breakfast with Nabile Farès." Nomadics blog entry September 2, 2016 (http://www.pierrejoris.com/blog/nabile-fares-1940-2016.)

"Abdellatif Laâbi : So many betweens!" Foreword to *In Praise of Defeat: Poems by Abdellatif Laâbi*, archipelago books, 2016.

"Fez: City through Time & Space." Talk given at *Chronopolis Conference*, University at Albany, March 23—24, 2007.

"On the Nomadic Circulation of Contemporary Poetics between Europe, North America & the Maghreb." first published in Carrie Noland & Barrett Watten, eds. Diasporic Poetics, Palgrave MacMillan, 2009. Reprinted in *Justifying the Margins*, Salt Publishers, 2009.

"Introduction to *Diwan Ifrikiya*." *The University of California Book of North African Literature*. Co-edited with Habib Tengour. University of

California Press as volume 4 in the *Poems For The Millennium* anthology series, 2012.

"*On Poetry & Miscegenation*: Interview by Orlando Reade." First published on the *Africa is a Country* site (https://africasacountry.com/2013/12/the-book-of-north-african-literature-pierre-joris-on-poetry-and-miscegenation/)

The various poetry inserts between the essays all come from *The University of California Book of North African Literature*. Pierre Joris & Habib Tengour. University of California Press, 2012.

"Snapshots" was published in *Revolution Goes Through Walls* by Safaa Fathy translated by Pierre Joris with Safaa Fathy. SplitLevel Texts, 2018

PIERRE JORIS has moved between Europe, the US & North Africa for over half a century now, publishing more than 50 books of poetry, essays, translations & anthologies—most recently:

Adonis & Pierre Joris, Conversations in the Pyrenees (CMP 2018); a translation of Egyptian poet Safaa Fathy's *Revolution Goes Through Walls* (SplitLevel, 2018), *The Book of U /Le livre des cormorans* (poems; with Nicole Peyrafitte, 2017); *The Agony of I.B.* (a play 2016); *An American Suite* (early poems; inpatient press 2016); *Barzakh: Poems 2000-2012* (Black Widow Press 2014); *Breathturn into Timestead: The Collected Later Poetry of Paul Celan* (FSG 2014); *A Voice full of Cities: The Collected Essays of Robert Kelly* (2014, Contra Mundum Press) & *The University of California Book of North African Literature* (volume 4 in the Poems for the Millennium series, coedited with Habib Tengour, 2012).

Forthcoming are the two final volumes of his Paul Celan translations, *Microliths* (Posthumous prose) from CMP (2019) & *The Collected Earlier Poetry* (FSG 2020), as well as a *Pierre Joris Reader* (BWP, 2020).

When not on the road, he lives in Bay Ridge, Brooklyn, with his wife, multimedia praticienne Nicole Peyrafitte.

www.ingramcontent.com/pod-product-compliance
Lightning Source LLC
Chambersburg PA
CBHW030112100526
44591CB00009B/371